Your Daily Dose of Mojo

Create an amazing year!

Theresa

ALSO BY THERESA ROSE

Opening the Kimono: A Woman's Intimate Journey Through Life's Biggest Challenges

Start Now, Grow Big

Bits of Bigness: Inspirational Nuggets to Remind You of Your Magnificence

Your Daily Dose of Mojo

365 Days of Mindful Living and Working

THERESA ROSE

Copyright © 2015 by Theresa Rose

All rights reserved. No part of this book may be used or reproduced in any manner whatsoever without written permission from the author except in the case of brief quotations included in critical articles and reviews.

Printed in the United States of America

First Printing 2015

ISBN-13: 978-0981886930

Serious Mojo Publications
Minneapolis, MN
TheresaRose.com

To order, visit TheresaRose.com or call 952-456-1670.
Bulk discounts available.

FOR JEAN

My strongest advocate, my greatest sounding board, and the very best friend in the whole wide world

INTRODUCTION

If you are struggling to stay happy amid the countless challenges at home, the ongoing stress at work, and the relentless effects of time, this book is for you.

You hold in your hands a powerful tool that will motivate, engage and inspire you to create the rich, joyful life you desire and deserve. Simply put, this daily inspirational book will boost your mojo and bring you back to bliss, both at home and in the workplace.

What is mojo? It's that fire, that energy, that zest that *makes life juicy*. If you've got your mojo working, you are on top of the world: energetic, creative, and fulfilled. If you've lost it, you may have to look up to see the bottom: depressed, tired, overwhelmed, and unable to accomplish much of anything. Mojo is our fuel that propels us toward our dreams, and its absence keeps us glued to the couch, watching life instead of living it.

This book is all about **being mindful of your thoughts and actions**. It will prompt deeper reflection, stir the soul, and compel substantive action that will truly make a difference in how you live your life both personally and professionally. Every dose of mojo is designed to build upon each other yet allows for spontaneous page-flipping to suit your mood and needs at the time. The words are simple, yet each message is profound in its potential impact on your daily behaviors and, ultimately, the life you are creating.

Your Daily Dose of Mojo is a relevant and timely book because our society is stressed now more than ever, and we are seeking more meaning in our work and lives. It's important to have this daily positive reminder of the power of our energy and the amazingness of life, despite the inevitable stresses we face. We are also extremely pressed for time. The daily lessons are short and to the point, allowing you to fit them in on-the-fly while at work, at home or on-the-go. This is a crucial book for our busy lives.

On every daily dose page, there are three journaling activities designed to bring you to a deeper state of mindfulness. Each set of exercises will enhance the teachings, create a focused action for the day, and encourage new habits. In addition to the inspirational message, there are three areas of self-reflection that you can use to stay focused on what you need to do to consciously create every day as you see fit. For optimal benefit, I recommend that you read a dose both in the morning and in the evening, and even find a few minutes throughout the day to review it. By immersing yourself in this wave of empowerment and transformation, you are getting into the driver's seat of your life, no matter what kind of crazy, wackadoo stress surrounds you.

Actions I Will Take Today to Boost My Mojo

This journal activity will help you set your intention every day so you can really commit to your goals and actions. By translating your thoughts onto the page, your ideas become more tangible, and therefore, more actionable. You will be acknowledging your intention and thus becoming more engaged in making it happen, day in and day out. I recommend you jot down what specific tasks you will take that are in alignment with the dose of the day. For example, you may write, "I will take at least ten minutes today to connect with my dear friend," or "I will take one specific action toward the project I have been avoiding." Your words will drive your actions, which in turn, will drive your day.

Gratitude Rant

This section entails writing down the things you are most thankful for instead of griping about the stress and challenges. It will allow you to flip your thinking to more positive and constructive thoughts that will impact your behaviors throughout the day.

If you are looking for the magic bullet that will make your life rich, full and abundant, look no further than the Gratitude Rant. When used on a daily basis, this simple but powerful presence tool will transform your life into the joyful romp it *is designed to be*.

Recall what it was like when you observed someone rant and rave about something. Typically there is a frenzy associated with it, almost as if she is "out of her mind." Well, that's the same kind of energy I encourage you to convey in your rant, but instead of being out of your mind, you will be *in your heart*.

Here's how it works: Take five minutes at the end of each day to unplug from the machines in your life—the TV, radio, computer, smartphone, and tablet—and arrive in the present moment. Take some deep cleansing breaths to get rid of the stress you have been lugging around. Clear your mind of everything on your to-do list. (You can pick it all back up later after the exercise, but you don't have to.)

Read your Daily Dose of Mojo and ask yourself, "What am I grateful for?" At first, your mind may scream at you, "NOTHING! Life is so hard! You have so much to do! Everything sucks!" But, keep at it. Ask yourself the question over and over again: What am I grateful for?

Start simple. Notice that you are grateful for your body,

your health, your home, and your loved ones. Then expand beyond those themes and let yourself feel gratitude for all of the big moments and the small victories, for the wonderful and not-so-wonderful things that have happened to you, recognizing that every single event has had some sort of positive impact on you. Sometimes our days show us what we do NOT want to re-create.

> *Be grateful* for music.
> *Be grateful* for laughter.
> *Be grateful* for cuddles with your kids or grandkids.
> *Be grateful* for the sun on your face.
> *Be grateful* for the meal you just consumed, and the person who prepared it.

Look around and notice how truly blessed you are. Let the gratitude come flowing out of you without judgment or deep introspection. Simply let the blessings bathe over you, one after the other after the other in rapid succession.

After just a few short minutes of performing a Gratitude Rant, you will notice that your stress levels have dramatically decreased. Your edges will be softened, and your anxieties will be replaced with a quiet sense of peace and joy. In short, you will have made the most important journey of your life: from your head to your heart.

Close your Gratitude Rant with a big breath of appreciation for the sacred moment you have just experienced, recognizing that you have the power within you to change your attitude, perspective, and ultimately your experience. Start ranting about your amazing life!

Personal Reflections

This is the section where you can share your feelings, fears, joys and other emotions that arise as a result of the daily mojo lesson. This activity creates a conscious connection between obstacles preventing you from taking action and what needs to happen to get through them. With awareness comes transformation, and your personal reflections will be the roadmap you will use to drive your life in the direction of your dreams.

Thank you for trusting in me to be your guide on the journey to your best year yet. As you walk this path with me every day, you will find *remarkable things unfolding* in every area of your life. In 365 days, you will become stronger, healthier, calmer, richer, and most importantly, more joyful than ever before. Let's get started.

1

Your life is meant to be filled with joy and laughter. *Boldly and brazenly* pursue them.

Actions I Will Take Today to Boost My Mojo:
_____
_____
_____
_____
_____

Gratitude Rant:
_____
_____
_____
_____
_____

Personal Reflections:
_____
_____
_____
_____
_____

2

Be generous with your smiles, as you will make someone's day while creating a meaningful life for yourself.

Actions I Will Take Today to Boost My Mojo:

Gratitude Rant:

Personal Reflections:

3

Relax into every moment so that stress will naturally melt away while true happiness emerges.

Actions I Will Take Today to Boost My Mojo:
_____
_____
_____
_____
_____

Gratitude Rant:
_____
_____
_____
_____
_____

Personal Reflections:
_____
_____
_____
_____
_____

4

Act childish today! Fill your day with fun and goofy moments.

Actions I Will Take Today to Boost My Mojo:

_____
_____
_____
_____
_____

Gratitude Rant:

_____
_____
_____
_____
_____

Personal Reflections:

_____
_____
_____
_____
_____

5

We aren't supposed to suffer. Anyone who tells you that nonsense is selling you something.

Actions I Will Take Today to Boost My Mojo:

___

Gratitude Rant:

___

Personal Reflections:

___

6

Drive your co-workers crazy today by radiating joy and lightness.

Actions I Will Take Today to Boost My Mojo:

Gratitude Rant:

Personal Reflections:

7

Be a *Joy Detective*—
look for fun in every situation you find yourself in today.

Actions I Will Take Today to Boost My Mojo:
___
___
___
___
___

Gratitude Rant:
___
___
___
___
___

Personal Reflections:
___
___
___
___
___

8

You can choose the day you are going to have and ultimately the life you are living. What will you choose to be, do, and have?

Actions I Will Take Today to Boost My Mojo:
___
___
___
___
___

Gratitude Rant:
___
___
___
___
___

Personal Reflections:
___
___
___
___
___

9

Ditch the Negative Nelly, boo-hoo, "I have-to" attitude that everyone else seems to be sporting, and embrace a fabulous "I get-to" reality instead.

Actions I Will Take Today to Boost My Mojo:

Gratitude Rant:

Personal Reflections:

10

Make today a Victim-Free Zone. Don't allow yourself to bemoan how terrible things are. If you don't like something, change it or change your attitude towards it. Easy peasy.

Actions I Will Take Today to Boost My Mojo:

Gratitude Rant:

Personal Reflections:

11

The right choices aren't hard to make. They are easy to make, but sometimes difficult to execute. Make the right choice, and then ask for help in getting you there.

Actions I Will Take Today to Boost My Mojo:
_____
_____
_____
_____
_____

Gratitude Rant:
_____
_____
_____
_____
_____

Personal Reflections:
_____
_____
_____
_____
_____

12

We often make things far more
complicated than they need to be.
Instead of blah-blah-blahing an issue to
death, simply make the choice
from your Higher Self,
and let go of the drama.

Actions I Will Take Today to Boost My Mojo:

_____
_____
_____
_____
_____

Gratitude Rant:

_____
_____
_____
_____
_____

Personal Reflections:

_____
_____
_____
_____
_____

13

You have everything you need to live a rich, thriving life. You may not have every last detail worked out yet, but you have the one thing that makes the difference between surviving and thriving: CHOICE.

Actions I Will Take Today to Boost My Mojo:
_____
_____
_____
_____
_____

Gratitude Rant:
_____
_____
_____
_____
_____

Personal Reflections:
_____
_____
_____
_____
_____

14

Choose to be the Best You today,
and watch the *beautiful results unfold.*

Actions I Will Take Today to Boost My Mojo:

Gratitude Rant:

Personal Reflections:

15

Your open heart is the doorway to peace, wisdom, and abundance.

Actions I Will Take Today to Boost My Mojo:
_____
_____
_____
_____
_____

Gratitude Rant:
_____
_____
_____
_____
_____

Personal Reflections:
_____
_____
_____
_____

# 16

Who needs to hear from you today? What acts of kindness can you perform?

Actions I Will Take Today to Boost My Mojo:

_____
_____
_____
_____
_____

Gratitude Rant:

_____
_____
_____
_____
_____

Personal Reflections:

_____
_____
_____
_____
_____

17

Tragedy and trauma are painful gifts
that allow us to step out of our own
story for a moment—
and then act from
a place of compassion.

Actions I Will Take Today to Boost My Mojo:
_____
_____
_____
_____
_____

Gratitude Rant:
_____
_____
_____
_____
_____

Personal Reflections:
_____
_____
_____
_____
_____

18

Show mercy for the unconscious goofballs in your life. They deserve your compassion, for they have forgotten how magnificent they are.

Actions I Will Take Today to Boost My Mojo:

___

Gratitude Rant:

___

Personal Reflections:

___

19

Seek out new opportunities today to selflessly give to another in need.

Actions I Will Take Today to Boost My Mojo:

Gratitude Rant:

Personal Reflections:

20

True understanding comes from that quiet, non-judgmental place in our hearts that knows everyone is Divine.

Actions I Will Take Today to Boost My Mojo:

_____
_____
_____
_____
_____

Gratitude Rant:

_____
_____
_____
_____
_____

Personal Reflections:

_____
_____
_____
_____
_____

21

Showing compassion to our loved ones is the easy part. The trick is showing it to the challenging ones. It is only then that we can truly live a life of peace.

Actions I Will Take Today to Boost My Mojo:
_____
_____
_____
_____
_____

Gratitude Rant:
_____
_____
_____
_____
_____

Personal Reflections:
_____
_____
_____
_____
_____

22

An Infinite Source is in radical support of you. Open to the Power of Spirit, and watch your dreams become reality.

Actions I Will Take Today to Boost My Mojo:

_____
_____
_____
_____
_____

Gratitude Rant:

_____
_____

_____
_____

Personal Reflections:

_____
_____
_____
_____
_____

23

You are more than a meat suit.
You have Spirit pulsating within you
and around you.

Actions I Will Take Today to Boost My Mojo:

Gratitude Rant:

Personal Reflections:

24

Your Higher Power is an Infinite Presence that is always available to you, and you can access it 24/7 through a quiet mind and open heart.

Actions I Will Take Today to Boost My Mojo:

_____
_____
_____
_____
_____

Gratitude Rant:

_____
_____
_____
_____
_____

Personal Reflections:

_____
_____
_____
_____
_____

25

Cultivating an authentic relationship with Spirit is one of the most powerful things you can do to create the rich, juicy life you desire and deserve.

Actions I Will Take Today to Boost My Mojo:

Gratitude Rant:

Personal Reflections:

26

Don't let anyone else tell you how to connect to Spirit. Your job is to interact with the Divine that feels in harmony with your beliefs and values.

Actions I Will Take Today to Boost My Mojo:
___
___
___
___
___

Gratitude Rant:
___
___
___
___
___

Personal Reflections:
___
___
___
___
___

27

Spirit can be found in the whisper of the wind, the laughter of a child, and the love in your heart. It is everywhere, and It is beautiful. Let It light your path.

Actions I Will Take Today to Boost My Mojo:
_____
_____
_____
_____
_____

Gratitude Rant:
_____
_____
_____
_____
_____

Personal Reflections:
_____
_____
_____
_____
_____

28

Spirit is more than a name, more than a dogma, and more than a religion.
It is a Divine Presence that gives meaning to our existence.
It is here to help us, not judge us.

Actions I Will Take Today to Boost My Mojo:

_____
_____
_____
_____
_____

Gratitude Rant:

_____
_____
_____
_____
_____

Personal Reflections:

_____
_____
_____
_____
_____

29

You become more powerful when you ground your energy into the Earth. Imagine your energetic roots plunging into the ground and wrapping themselves around the core of the planet. This simple technique will bring you peace and tranquility.

Actions I Will Take Today to Boost My Mojo:

_____
_____
_____
_____
_____

Gratitude Rant:

_____
_____
_____
_____
_____

Personal Reflections:

_____
_____
_____
_____
_____

30

We get stressed and crazy when our energy bounces around our heads like a pinball machine. The next time you feel stressed out, slow down and breathe into your legs. It will unplug the arcade game in your head.

Actions I Will Take Today to Boost My Mojo:

Gratitude Rant:

Personal Reflections:

31

Trees grow only when they have a strong root structure, and we grow only when we have our roots firmly planted.

Actions I Will Take Today to Boost My Mojo:

Gratitude Rant:

Personal Reflections:

32

When life gets overwhelming, get down and dirty. It's amazing what a little outdoor time can do to cut out the crazy. *Get out there and play.*

Actions I Will Take Today to Boost My Mojo:

Gratitude Rant:

Personal Reflections:

33

You cannot create a life of Bigness
without a firm foundation. Focus on
planting your feet firmly on the ground,
both literally and figuratively,
and you will create
a solid framework for success.

Actions I Will Take Today to Boost My Mojo:

Gratitude Rant:

Personal Reflections:

34

Let the gravitational pull of the Earth hold you in a state of security, safety, and comfort. The Earth provides you with all of the essentials
you need to survive, and it can also help you to thrive.

Actions I Will Take Today to Boost My Mojo:

_____
_____
_____
_____
_____

Gratitude Rant:

_____
_____
_____
_____
_____

Personal Reflections:

_____
_____
_____
_____
_____

35

Be a lightening rod of goodness! Send your powerful juju into the Earth through your conscious intention, and you'll be able to share more of it with the world.

Actions I Will Take Today to Boost My Mojo:

Gratitude Rant:

Personal Reflections:

YOUR DAILY DOSE OF MOJO

36

You have the power within you to create a rich, rewarding life. Let your vision guide your actions.

Actions I Will Take Today to Boost My Mojo:

Gratitude Rant:

Personal Reflections:

37

When your energy is depleted, you can't pursue your passions. Recharge your batteries through conscious breathing, inspired movement, or some good old-fashioned rest.

Actions I Will Take Today to Boost My Mojo:

_____
_____
_____
_____
_____

Gratitude Rant:

_____
_____
_____
_____
_____

Personal Reflections:

_____
_____
_____
_____

38

Energy comes in many forms: physical, mental, emotional, spiritual, monetary, creative, and collaborative, to name a few. If you are lacking in one, boost the others to help nudge you back into balance.

Actions I Will Take Today to Boost My Mojo:

_____
_____
_____
_____
_____

Gratitude Rant:

_____
_____
_____
_____
_____

Personal Reflections:

_____
_____
_____
_____
_____

39

You are an energy depot, receiving, assimilating, and transmitting it at all times. The energy you take in affects the energy you send out, so make sure that you let in only those forces that are in your highest good.

Actions I Will Take Today to Boost My Mojo:

Gratitude Rant:

Personal Reflections:

40

Energy is the fuel you use to consciously create your life. Be diligent about keeping your tank full of the highest quality fuel so you can get to your dream destinations *while enjoying the journey.*

Actions I Will Take Today to Boost My Mojo:
_____
_____
_____
_____
_____

Gratitude Rant:
_____
_____
_____
_____
_____

Personal Reflections:
_____
_____
_____
_____
_____

41

Don't settle for a life of stress, exhaustion, and missed opportunities. Spend your energy wisely, delegate responsibly, and let go of the need to be perfect. You deserve to have some mojo left over for YOU.

Actions I Will Take Today to Boost My Mojo:
_____
_____
_____
_____
_____

Gratitude Rant:
_____
_____
_____
_____
_____

Personal Reflections:
_____
_____
_____
_____
_____

42

Take ownership of your daily energetic requirements. Just as you make sure that you get enough nutrients, water and rest (hopefully!), so too should you make sure that you feed your energy tank with movement, meditation, and Mother Nature.

Actions I Will Take Today to Boost My Mojo:

_____
_____
_____
_____
_____

Gratitude Rant:

_____
_____
_____
_____
_____

Personal Reflections:

_____
_____
_____
_____
_____

43

Gratitude is one of the most powerful tools of transformation available to you. It is the rocket booster that will catapult your dreams into reality.

Actions I Will Take Today to Boost My Mojo:
_____
_____
_____
_____
_____

Gratitude Rant:
_____
_____
_____
_____
_____

Personal Reflections:
_____
_____
_____
_____
_____

44

Start and end each day with a quick gratitude rant, allowing you to bathe in all that is wonderful in your life. Feel your heart expand as you acknowledge how rich your life is.

Actions I Will Take Today to Boost My Mojo:

Gratitude Rant:

Personal Reflections:

45

Are you also grateful for the yucky stuff in your life? Everything contains a gift, and it is your job to dig for it.

Actions I Will Take Today to Boost My Mojo:
_____
_____
_____
_____
_____

Gratitude Rant:
_____
_____
_____
_____
_____

Personal Reflections:
_____
_____
_____
_____
_____

46

You don't have to be grateful FOR a painful experience, but you can be grateful IN it. Grace can be found in a genuine, humble practice of gratitude.

Actions I Will Take Today to Boost My Mojo:

Gratitude Rant:

Personal Reflections:

47

Whenever you feel down, depressed, or angry, ask yourself a simple question: "What am I grateful for in this moment?" It will shift your energy and get you out of the darkness.

Actions I Will Take Today to Boost My Mojo:
_____
_____
_____
_____
_____

Gratitude Rant:
_____
_____
_____
_____
_____

Personal Reflections:
_____
_____
_____
_____
_____

48

If you aren't grateful for anything, you aren't trying hard enough. You woke up this morning, and you are reading this. Countless gifts are contained within those simple acts alone.

Actions I Will Take Today to Boost My Mojo:

Gratitude Rant:

Personal Reflections:

49

Be grateful for your loved ones. Be grateful for the experiences. Be grateful for the lessons. Be grateful for the victories and the losses. It's all good.

Actions I Will Take Today to Boost My Mojo:

Gratitude Rant:

Personal Reflections:

YOUR DAILY DOSE OF MOJO

50

Sacredness is found in the stillness. Before you start the endless wave of "doing" today, just BE for a bit.

Actions I Will Take Today to Boost My Mojo:
_____
_____
_____
_____
_____

Gratitude Rant:
_____
_____
_____
_____
_____

Personal Reflections:
_____
_____
_____
_____
_____

51

Our troubles live in the future. We may not have everything we want exactly as we want it, but we can choose to be present and grateful NOW.
Let the worrying happen in the future.

Actions I Will Take Today to Boost My Mojo:

Gratitude Rant:

Personal Reflections:

52

Joy lives in the present. Relax your body, quiet your mind, and breathe. Let your concerns melt away. You are here now, and life is good.

Actions I Will Take Today to Boost My Mojo:

_____
_____
_____
_____
_____

Gratitude Rant:

_____
_____
_____
_____
_____

Personal Reflections:

_____
_____
_____
_____
_____

53

The past holds our memories, and the future holds our longings and fears. The present holds the key to the magic kingdom of joy and peace.

Actions I Will Take Today to Boost My Mojo:

_____
_____
_____
_____
_____

Gratitude Rant:

_____
_____
_____
_____
_____

Personal Reflections:

_____
_____
_____
_____
_____

54

In this moment, everything is happening exactly as it should. Breathe into this sacred space where you are fully present with what is.

Actions I Will Take Today to Boost My Mojo:

_____
_____
_____
_____
_____

Gratitude Rant:

_____
_____
_____
_____
_____

Personal Reflections:

_____
_____
_____
_____
_____

55

Arrive fully in the moment—physically, mentally, emotionally, and spiritually. Don't linger in the past, and don't fast forward into the future. All you have is now. Be here for it.

Actions I Will Take Today to Boost My Mojo:
_____
_____
_____
_____
_____

Gratitude Rant:
_____
_____
_____
_____
_____

Personal Reflections:
_____
_____
_____
_____
_____

56

Even if something is uncomfortable or painful, don't check out or escape. Be present in the experience, and seek out the gifts. By doing so, you will never have another "bad" day in your life.

Actions I Will Take Today to Boost My Mojo:

_____
_____
_____
_____
_____

Gratitude Rant:

_____
_____
_____
_____
_____

Personal Reflections:

_____
_____
_____
_____
_____

57

Your body is the only one you are going to get this time around. Treat it well, both inside and out. What can you do today to care for yourself?

Actions I Will Take Today to Boost My Mojo:

Gratitude Rant:

Personal Reflections:

58

The food you eat is like the gas you put in your car. Are you giving yourself nutrient-rich fuel, or are you starving yourself by putting junk in your tank? Make one better food choice today, and see how much better you feel.

Actions I Will Take Today to Boost My Mojo:

Gratitude Rant:

Personal Reflections:

59

Get tuned into what your entire body needs in order to be as healthy as possible. Don't let those pesky little taste buds be the sole decision-makers. Consult your colon! Ask your heart! Check in with your stomach!

Actions I Will Take Today to Boost My Mojo:

Gratitude Rant:

Personal Reflections:

60

Our health is the one thing we can't live without. At the end of our lives, we won't be obsessing over money, tasks, or possessions. Let's honor this journey and be good to our bodies so we can enjoy a nice, long ride.

Actions I Will Take Today to Boost My Mojo:

Gratitude Rant:

Personal Reflections:

61

If you are exhausted, rest. If you are hungry, eat. If you are thirsty, drink. If you are stiff, move. The recipes are easy, but we've got to take action and choose the finest ingredients.

Actions I Will Take Today to Boost My Mojo:

_____
_____
_____
_____
_____

Gratitude Rant:

_____
_____
_____
_____
_____

Personal Reflections:

_____
_____
_____
_____
_____

62

It's never too late to make a positive choice. Transformation happens one conscious choice at a time. If you want to improve your health, do one more thing in support of it and one less thing that undermines it.

Actions I Will Take Today to Boost My Mojo:

_____
_____
_____
_____
_____

Gratitude Rant:

_____
_____
_____
_____
_____

Personal Reflections:

_____
_____
_____
_____
_____

63

You'll never have perfect health or the perfect body. But that doesn't mean you should accept the status quo. Come up with realistic goals, and take inspired action to get you there. *You really can* feel better than ever before.

Actions I Will Take Today to Boost My Mojo:
_____
_____
_____
_____
_____

Gratitude Rant:
_____
_____
_____
_____
_____

Personal Reflections:
_____
_____
_____
_____
_____

64

Wanting something isn't good enough; we need to summon the will to take action.

Actions I Will Take Today to Boost My Mojo:

___
___
___
___
___

Gratitude Rant:

___
___
___
___
___

Personal Reflections:

___
___
___
___
___

65

Strengthen your will by making a short list of impactful things you can do in support of your dream. Schedule when you will do them—and then DO them.

Actions I Will Take Today to Boost My Mojo:

_____
_____
_____
_____
_____

Gratitude Rant:

_____
_____
_____
_____
_____

Personal Reflections:

_____
_____
_____
_____
_____

66

The difference between the people in the spotlight and those in the bleachers is that the ones in the spotlight kept working at it even when it was unpleasant. Keep going. It's worth it.

Actions I Will Take Today to Boost My Mojo:

Gratitude Rant:

Personal Reflections:

67

Be disciplined in your quest for a happier, more abundant life. Wake up a little earlier. Work when you don't want to. Make that last call. Going the extra mile will pay off in the long run.

Actions I Will Take Today to Boost My Mojo:
_____
_____
_____
_____
_____

Gratitude Rant:
_____
_____
_____
_____
_____

Personal Reflections:
_____
_____
_____
_____

68

Don't be a Scarlett O'Hara and say "Fiddle dee dee. I'll think about it tomorrow." If you want a better life, do something in support of it NOW.

Actions I Will Take Today to Boost My Mojo:
_____
_____
_____
_____
_____

Gratitude Rant:
_____
_____
_____
_____
_____

Personal Reflections:
_____
_____
_____
_____
_____

69

Lethargy and inertia will Pac-man your life away, one moment at a time. Decide the steps you can take to create the life you want, and tap into your reserves of will to do them each and every day.

Actions I Will Take Today to Boost My Mojo:

Gratitude Rant:

Personal Reflections:

70

Live an Excuse-Free Life. Don't let yourself off the hook by listing all of the reasons why you can't do something. You will either do it or your won't. The rest of the narrative is just theatre.

Actions I Will Take Today to Boost My Mojo:
___
___
___
___
___

Gratitude Rant:
___
___
___
___
___

Personal Reflections:
___
___
___
___
___

71

You are a magnificent being worthy of great love, joy and abundance!

Actions I Will Take Today to Boost My Mojo:

Gratitude Rant:

Personal Reflections:

72

So what if you have wrinkles, jiggles, lumps, and bumps? You are a beautiful person inside and out, and don't let anyone tell you otherwise.

Actions I Will Take Today to Boost My Mojo:

Gratitude Rant:

Personal Reflections:

73

It's far too common to obsess over our flaws. Instead, choose to be different, and focus on your countless positive qualities.

Actions I Will Take Today to Boost My Mojo:

Gratitude Rant:

Personal Reflections:

74

We can't all be Jennifer Aniston. Let's decide to honor and appreciate ourselves *as-is*. There is beauty and grace in authenticity.

Actions I Will Take Today to Boost My Mojo:

_____
_____
_____
_____
_____

Gratitude Rant:

_____
_____
_____
_____
_____

Personal Reflections:

_____
_____
_____
_____
_____

75

Stuart Smalley was right: You ARE good enough, you ARE smart enough, and doggonit, people DO like you!

Actions I Will Take Today to Boost My Mojo:
_____
_____
_____
_____
_____

Gratitude Rant:
_____
_____
_____
_____
_____

Personal Reflections:
_____
_____
_____
_____
_____

76

Nothing about owning our awesomeness is arrogant or boastful. We are teaching others by modeling healthy self-esteem.

Actions I Will Take Today to Boost My Mojo:

_____
_____
_____
_____
_____

Gratitude Rant:

_____
_____
_____
_____
_____

Personal Reflections:

_____
_____
_____
_____
_____

77

See yourself as the gorgeous, powerful, amazing person *that you are*. When you do, others will begin to see you in the same light.

Actions I Will Take Today to Boost My Mojo:

Gratitude Rant:

Personal Reflections:

78

Spirit is the ultimate gift giver, and all we need to do is open our hearts and arms wide to receive it.

Actions I Will Take Today to Boost My Mojo:

Gratitude Rant:

Personal Reflections:

79

We all know the famous line, "Ask and ye shall receive." Remember, we need to actually accept the blessing when it is presented to us.

Actions I Will Take Today to Boost My Mojo:

Gratitude Rant:

Personal Reflections:

80

When we say "YES" to the Universe when it presents us with an opportunity to live our dream, more opportunities will automatically emerge. If we say "NO," then the well will eventually dry up. SAY YES!

Actions I Will Take Today to Boost My Mojo:

Gratitude Rant:

Personal Reflections:

81

There is more than enough to go around. We don't need to be stingy or frugal, nor do we need to get passed over. It is our right to receive.

Actions I Will Take Today to Boost My Mojo:
_____
_____
_____
_____
_____

Gratitude Rant:
_____
_____
_____
_____
_____

Personal Reflections:
_____
_____
_____
_____
_____

82

Spirit provides all of the guidance, wisdom, support, and healing that we need. Graciously accepting it is simply fulfilling our end of the bargain.

Actions I Will Take Today to Boost My Mojo:

Gratitude Rant:

Personal Reflections:

83

Be open to receiving the answer to your prayers, even if it doesn't resemble what you thought it would look like. Sometimes the greatest gifts we receive are wrapped in unusual, unexpected packages.

Actions I Will Take Today to Boost My Mojo:

Gratitude Rant:

Personal Reflections:

84

Don't ever say, "You shouldn't have!" when someone gives you something. Instead, be thankful, be gracious, and be open to receiving even more.

Actions I Will Take Today to Boost My Mojo:

Gratitude Rant:

Personal Reflections:

85

Dreams are merely a state of pre-reality. Dream big, and take action in support of your vision.

Actions I Will Take Today to Boost My Mojo:

_____
_____
_____
_____
_____

Gratitude Rant:

_____
_____
_____
_____
_____

Personal Reflections:

_____
_____
_____
_____
_____

86

What do you want in your life? What are your health goals? How do you want to spend your time? How much money do you want? What relationships do you want to enjoy? You can't get it before you dream it.

Actions I Will Take Today to Boost My Mojo:

Gratitude Rant:

Personal Reflections:

87

Do the math:
You CAN have the life of your dreams.
Imagination + Execution = Realization

Actions I Will Take Today to Boost My Mojo:
_____
_____
_____
_____
_____

Gratitude Rant:
_____
_____
_____
_____
_____

Personal Reflections:
_____
_____
_____
_____
_____

88

No dream is too big, because there is no limit to the manifestation power contained within you and the Universe.

Actions I Will Take Today to Boost My Mojo:

Gratitude Rant:

Personal Reflections:

89

Relentlessly pursue YOUR dream each and every day, and ditch the faux-dreams of others. If your passion isn't there, you won't manifest it anyway. Make it yours and yours alone.

Actions I Will Take Today to Boost My Mojo:

Gratitude Rant:

Personal Reflections:

90

Write your dream down in such a way that you can memorize it and recite it every single day. When it continually stays top of mind, it will begin to take form physically.

Actions I Will Take Today to Boost My Mojo:
_____
_____
_____
_____
_____

Gratitude Rant:
_____
_____
_____
_____
_____

Personal Reflections:
_____
_____
_____
_____
_____

91

Live from the perspective of your dream. Act as if it is already happening. Vibrate at its frequency. Soon you will discover that you have attained it.

Actions I Will Take Today to Boost My Mojo:

Gratitude Rant:

Personal Reflections:

92

Only you can create the life you desire, and it doesn't come magically. You must take action if you want to live a life by design instead of one by default.

Actions I Will Take Today to Boost My Mojo:
_____
_____
_____
_____
_____

Gratitude Rant:
_____
_____
_____
_____
_____

Personal Reflections:
_____
_____
_____
_____
_____

93

Sometimes taking the smallest action will be the catalyst needed to create forward momentum towards realizing your dream.

Actions I Will Take Today to Boost My Mojo:
_____
_____
_____
_____
_____

Gratitude Rant:
_____
_____
_____
_____
_____

Personal Reflections:
_____
_____
_____
_____
_____

94

Don't judge yourself by the outcomes of your actions, but hold yourself accountable for taking them.

Actions I Will Take Today to Boost My Mojo:

_____
_____
_____
_____
_____

Gratitude Rant:

_____
_____
_____
_____

Personal Reflections:

_____
_____
_____
_____
_____

95

One of my favorite quotes is from none other than Yoda: "Do or do not. There is no try." Just do it already, and don't worry about trying.

Actions I Will Take Today to Boost My Mojo:

_____
_____
_____
_____
_____

Gratitude Rant:

_____
_____
_____
_____
_____

Personal Reflections:

_____
_____
_____
_____
_____

96

A step forward, even if it's the wrong step, is a step forward. The enemy of your dream is inertia.

Actions I Will Take Today to Boost My Mojo:
_____
_____
_____
_____
_____

Gratitude Rant:
_____
_____
_____
_____
_____

Personal Reflections:
_____
_____
_____
_____
_____

97

An action becomes an inspired action when your intuition is guiding you, and your joy sustains you. Inspired actions will pave the way to your dream.

Actions I Will Take Today to Boost My Mojo:
_____
_____
_____
_____

Gratitude Rant:
_____
_____
_____
_____

Personal Reflections:
_____
_____
_____
_____

98

No one ever did anything great by sitting on the couch all day. Get up, get moving, and get BIG.
The world is waiting!

Actions I Will Take Today to Boost My Mojo:

Gratitude Rant:

Personal Reflections:

99

You deserve abundance in all things, not because of what you do, but because of *who you are*.

Actions I Will Take Today to Boost My Mojo:

_____
_____
_____
_____
_____

Gratitude Rant:

_____
_____
_____
_____
_____

Personal Reflections:

_____
_____
_____
_____
_____

YOUR DAILY DOSE OF MOJO

100

Someone somewhere might have told you that you don't deserve greatness. Guess what? He LIED. Either that or he was clueless as to how the Universe works. In any case, decide today to throw that toxic thought away for good.

Actions I Will Take Today to Boost My Mojo:

_____
_____
_____
_____
_____

Gratitude Rant:

_____
_____
_____
_____
_____

Personal Reflections:

_____
_____
_____
_____
_____

101

Nothing is admirable about martyrdom. Spirit wants you to live juicy and accept every last nugget of awesome that is coming your way. You deserve it.

Actions I Will Take Today to Boost My Mojo:

_____
_____
_____
_____
_____

Gratitude Rant:

_____
_____
_____
_____
_____

Personal Reflections:

_____
_____
_____
_____
_____

102

You are worthy of a life so well lived and a heart so well loved that others could write songs, poems, and plays about the magnificence *that is you*.

Actions I Will Take Today to Boost My Mojo:

Gratitude Rant:

Personal Reflections:

103

You are a child of Spirit, and the natural inheritor of all that is good and beautiful. Your worth is embedded in your essence.

Actions I Will Take Today to Boost My Mojo:

Gratitude Rant:

Personal Reflections:

104

Your ability to receive abundance is directly proportional to your level of self-worth. See yourself worthy of great blessings, and you will begin to receive them.

Actions I Will Take Today to Boost My Mojo:

Gratitude Rant:

Personal Reflections:

105

No accomplishment, accolade, reward, or blessing is above you. You deserve all that is fabulous.

Actions I Will Take Today to Boost My Mojo:

_____
_____
_____
_____
_____

Gratitude Rant:

_____
_____
_____
_____
_____

Personal Reflections:

_____
_____
_____
_____
_____

106

Spirit is here for you, every moment of every day. You can trust in this.

Actions I Will Take Today to Boost My Mojo:

_____
_____
_____
_____
_____

Gratitude Rant:

_____
_____
_____
_____
_____

Personal Reflections:

_____
_____
_____
_____
_____

107

Every question has an answer if you know how to ask it of Spirit. Get quiet, ask your question, and wait for the answer—which could take moments or days. Trust in the answer.

Actions I Will Take Today to Boost My Mojo:

Gratitude Rant:

Personal Reflections:

YOUR DAILY DOSE OF MOJO

108

By trusting in the fact that everything happens exactly as it should and in accordance with your highest good, your life becomes a lot more enjoyable.

Actions I Will Take Today to Boost My Mojo:

Gratitude Rant:

Personal Reflections:

109

Trust that you are in the perfect place at the perfect time to help co-create your perfect life. Divine timing is in force.

Actions I Will Take Today to Boost My Mojo:

_____
_____
_____
_____
_____

Gratitude Rant:

_____
_____
_____
_____
_____

Personal Reflections:

_____
_____
_____
_____
_____

YOUR DAILY DOSE OF MOJO

110

Second-guessing wastes precious energy. Trust that you are on the right path and things are unfolding exactly as planned.

Actions I Will Take Today to Boost My Mojo:

Gratitude Rant:

Personal Reflections:

111

A great deal of comfort can be found in the knowing that you are never, ever alone. You can trust in the power and presence of Spirit.

Actions I Will Take Today to Boost My Mojo:

_____
_____
_____
_____
_____

Gratitude Rant:

_____
_____
_____
_____
_____

Personal Reflections:

_____
_____
_____
_____
_____

112

The more you grow your ability to trust
and be vulnerable,
the bigger you will become.

Actions I Will Take Today to Boost My Mojo:

Gratitude Rant:

Personal Reflections:

113

When was the last time you received a massage or facial? What are you waiting for? It's time to care for yourself as much as you care for others.

Actions I Will Take Today to Boost My Mojo:
_____
_____
_____
_____
_____

Gratitude Rant:
_____
_____
_____
_____
_____

Personal Reflections:
_____
_____
_____
_____
_____

114

If you don't care for yourself, you are not serving others as well as you could. Self-care is a selfless, considerate act, not one to avoid.

Actions I Will Take Today to Boost My Mojo:

Gratitude Rant:

Personal Reflections:

115

Soak in a luxurious bath tonight. Not only will your body thank you, your spirit will too. Nothing says "I love myself" quite like a lavender bubble bath!

Actions I Will Take Today to Boost My Mojo:

Gratitude Rant:

Personal Reflections:

116

Make sure that you carve out some time today just for you. Be generous with yourself. You give to so many, and it's important that you give to yourself too.

Actions I Will Take Today to Boost My Mojo:

Gratitude Rant:

Personal Reflections:

117

Create a Self-care Toolkit of all of the things you can do to pamper and love yourself up. Have it at the ready for those times when you feel overwhelmed.

Actions I Will Take Today to Boost My Mojo:
_____
_____
_____
_____
_____

Gratitude Rant:
_____
_____
_____
_____
_____

Personal Reflections:
_____
_____
_____
_____
_____

118

Nothing is honorable or attractive about constantly ignoring one's needs. It only cuts off the flow of abundance, and makes life a lot more painful.
Be good to yourself!

Actions I Will Take Today to Boost My Mojo:

Gratitude Rant:

Personal Reflections:

119

Performing acts of self-care demonstrate to the Universe and all of those around you that you honor yourself. Creating that positive energy will attract other wonderful things to you.

Actions I Will Take Today to Boost My Mojo:

Gratitude Rant:

Personal Reflections:

YOUR DAILY DOSE OF MOJO

120

Honoring healthy boundaries will help you live happier, healthier, and more abundantly.

Actions I Will Take Today to Boost My Mojo:

Gratitude Rant:

Personal Reflections:

121

Don't let anyone walk all over you, either in person or online. It's OK to say that it isn't OK.

Actions I Will Take Today to Boost My Mojo:
_____
_____
_____
_____
_____

Gratitude Rant:
_____
_____
_____
_____
_____

Personal Reflections:
_____
_____
_____
_____
_____

122

One of the keys to success is to allow yourself to energetically grow as big as possible without allowing those around you to prey on your energy. Draw distinct boundaries between where you end—and where they begin.

Actions I Will Take Today to Boost My Mojo:
_____
_____
_____
_____
_____

Gratitude Rant:
_____
_____
_____
_____
_____

Personal Reflections:
_____
_____
_____
_____
_____

123

Don't own what isn't yours to own.

Actions I Will Take Today to Boost My Mojo:

Gratitude Rant:

Personal Reflections:

124

Get quiet and centered. Ask your Higher Self if anyone is energetically connected with you against your wishes. If you get a "Yes," imagine cutting the cord and taking back any energy she has siphoned from you. No one can take your energy from you.

Actions I Will Take Today to Boost My Mojo:

Gratitude Rant:

Personal Reflections:

125

Just as you don't want others to violate your boundaries, so too should you honor the boundaries of others. If you feel like you are crossing the line with someone, you probably are. Cut the cord, and ask yourself why you made that choice.

Actions I Will Take Today to Boost My Mojo:

Gratitude Rant:

Personal Reflections:

126

No one can make you feel a certain way. You have total autonomy to choose your experience. Do not let anyone else take the controls.

Actions I Will Take Today to Boost My Mojo:

Gratitude Rant:

Personal Reflections:

127

We all have wounds that need to be healed. There is power in having the courage to own our healing process.

Actions I Will Take Today to Boost My Mojo:

Gratitude Rant:

Personal Reflections:

128

Healing doesn't have to involve wallowing in all of the bad stuff that has happened. With the help of the right practitioner, we can learn from our traumas and grow stronger because of them.

Actions I Will Take Today to Boost My Mojo:

Gratitude Rant:

Personal Reflections:

129

The healing path has many roads. Find the one that speaks strongly to you, and trust that you will find peace and comfort when you come through the other side.

Actions I Will Take Today to Boost My Mojo:

Gratitude Rant:

Personal Reflections:

YOUR DAILY DOSE OF MOJO

130

Healing isn't for sissies! It often brings with it feelings of discomfort. If it were easy, we would have already moved through it by now. Be patient and stick with it. Don't give up.

Actions I Will Take Today to Boost My Mojo:

Gratitude Rant:

Personal Reflections:

131

What books, classes, workshops, retreats, or teachers are calling to you? What healing gifts are being nudged toward you? Take the plunge and work on getting out the gunk.

Actions I Will Take Today to Boost My Mojo:
___
___
___
___

Gratitude Rant:
___
___
___
___

Personal Reflections:
___
___
___
___

132

We never arrive at a point where everything has been "fixed." Fixed is a fantasy. Instead, be diligent about becoming the healthiest, most conscious person you can be.

Actions I Will Take Today to Boost My Mojo:

_____
_____
_____
_____
_____

Gratitude Rant:

_____
_____
_____
_____
_____

Personal Reflections:

_____
_____
_____
_____
_____

133

We can't make other people heal. We can only heal ourselves, model what it looks like to own our experiences, and support them if and/or when they are ready.

Actions I Will Take Today to Boost My Mojo:

Gratitude Rant:

Personal Reflections:

YOUR DAILY DOSE OF MOJO

134

Meditation is the quiet center where you discover the True You.

Actions I Will Take Today to Boost My Mojo:

Gratitude Rant:

Personal Reflections:

135

There are a lot of forms of meditation: transcendental, conscious breathing, walking, and even hooping! Find the version that is right for you, and watch your life transform.

Actions I Will Take Today to Boost My Mojo:
_____
_____
_____
_____
_____

Gratitude Rant:
_____
_____
_____
_____
_____

Personal Reflections:
_____
_____
_____
_____

136

Meditation is like taking a free vacation. Why wouldn't you want to have that blissful respite each and every day?

Actions I Will Take Today to Boost My Mojo:

Gratitude Rant:

Personal Reflections:

137

It has been said that prayer is when we ask for something, and meditation is when we listen. Let the practice of meditation strengthen your listening skills so you can act on the guidance you will invariably receive.

Actions I Will Take Today to Boost My Mojo:
_____
_____
_____
_____
_____

Gratitude Rant:
_____
_____
_____
_____
_____

Personal Reflections:
_____
_____
_____
_____
_____

YOUR DAILY DOSE OF MOJO

138

Sacred moments are created in the simple act of sitting in silence.

Actions I Will Take Today to Boost My Mojo:

Gratitude Rant:

Personal Reflections:

139

Don't make meditation a task with rigid rules or structure. It should be a joyful experience that you *get to do*. Give yourself the gift of meditation.

Actions I Will Take Today to Boost My Mojo:

_____
_____
_____
_____
_____

Gratitude Rant:

_____
_____
_____
_____
_____

Personal Reflections:

_____
_____
_____
_____
_____

140

As you sit in silence, let your thoughts bathe over you. Don't get attached to them, and don't try to stop thinking of them. Instead, let them waft through you with ease. You will be training yourself in the powerful practice of detachment.

Actions I Will Take Today to Boost My Mojo:

Gratitude Rant:

Personal Reflections:

141

Your environment impacts your ascension to greatness. Surround yourself only with those things and people that are in support of you.

Actions I Will Take Today to Boost My Mojo:

Gratitude Rant:

Personal Reflections:

142

Do your surroundings nurture you or nag at you? Look around and see where you can add more beauty and bliss. While you are at it, get rid of the things that are not-so-quietly mocking you. It's time *to clean house*.

Actions I Will Take Today to Boost My Mojo:

Gratitude Rant:

Personal Reflections:

143

Music can help create an environment of joy, gratitude, and growth. Let your favorite sounds, songs, and songbirds paint the ever-expanding landscape of your life.

Actions I Will Take Today to Boost My Mojo:
_____
_____
_____
_____
_____

Gratitude Rant:
_____
_____
_____
_____
_____

Personal Reflections:
_____
_____
_____
_____
_____

144

There's something about relaxing at the end of a long day in a quiet space filled with beauty and tranquility. Unplug from the noise of technology for a while, and let your system reset. You will be refreshed for another big day.

Actions I Will Take Today to Boost My Mojo:
_____
_____
_____
_____
_____

Gratitude Rant:
_____
_____
_____
_____
_____

Personal Reflections:
_____
_____
_____
_____
_____

145

Post notes of encouragement where you can regularly see them. If you are working on improving your self-esteem, put a sticky note on the bathroom mirror that says, "I am magnificent!" Let your environment work in concert with you in support of your dreams.

Actions I Will Take Today to Boost My Mojo:

___

Gratitude Rant:

___

Personal Reflections:

___

146

Are you in a supportive environment or a toxic one? How you can start making changes to improve the energy? Unplug from the drama of others. Clear the clutter. Brighten up the space. Do whatever it takes to shift it to something that has a positive impact.

Actions I Will Take Today to Boost My Mojo:

Gratitude Rant:

Personal Reflections:

147

If you want to supercharge your dreams, turn off the TV and turn on to Spirit. Energize your space with sacredness, beauty, and power. Remove anything that keeps you small or makes you feel icky. Your space can be a catalyst or a cage. Which one will you choose?

Actions I Will Take Today to Boost My Mojo:

Gratitude Rant:

Personal Reflections:

YOUR DAILY DOSE OF MOJO

148

When we truly take ownership of our lives, we let go of the mantle of "victim" that has kept us small.

Actions I Will Take Today to Boost My Mojo:

_____
_____
_____
_____
_____

Gratitude Rant:

_____
_____
_____
_____
_____

Personal Reflections:

_____
_____
_____
_____
_____

149

To own our choices
is to craft our lives.

Actions I Will Take Today to Boost My Mojo:
___

Gratitude Rant:
___

Personal Reflections:
___

150

You do not "have" to do a single thing. You "get" to do them. You own your experiences; they are not foisted upon you.

Actions I Will Take Today to Boost My Mojo:

Gratitude Rant:

Personal Reflections:

151

When we take ownership of our experiences, we take back our power from those who we previously perceived to be the cause of our pain.

Actions I Will Take Today to Boost My Mojo:
_____
_____
_____
_____
_____

Gratitude Rant:
_____
_____
_____
_____
_____

Personal Reflections:
_____
_____
_____
_____
_____

152

You can't protect yourself from pain, discomfort, betrayal, or abandonment. But you can own your reaction to them.

Actions I Will Take Today to Boost My Mojo:

Gratitude Rant:

Personal Reflections:

153

You are in charge. You own how your day will unfold. Don't allow anyone to hijack your joy.

Actions I Will Take Today to Boost My Mojo:

Gratitude Rant:

Personal Reflections:

154

Hold the deed to your days and the lease on your life. Own your successes, your shortcomings, and everything in between. You decide how your life will unfold.

Actions I Will Take Today to Boost My Mojo:

Gratitude Rant:

Personal Reflections:

155

Judging ourselves and others is a sure path to depression and disappointment.

Actions I Will Take Today to Boost My Mojo:

Gratitude Rant:

Personal Reflections:

156

You don't have to condone someone's poor choices, but you don't have to judge them either. Let others decide how they will walk in the world.

Actions I Will Take Today to Boost My Mojo:

_____
_____
_____
_____
_____

Gratitude Rant:

_____
_____
_____
_____
_____

Personal Reflections:

_____
_____
_____
_____
_____

157

How much of your precious energy has been wasted worrying about the actions of others? Was your worrying effective in changing them? Doubtful. Compassion and acceptance are better uses of your valuable time.

Actions I Will Take Today to Boost My Mojo:
_____
_____
_____
_____
_____

Gratitude Rant:
_____
_____
_____
_____
_____

Personal Reflections:
_____
_____
_____
_____
_____

158

Grace can be found in the moment where we genuinely and lovingly accept others exactly as they are.

Actions I Will Take Today to Boost My Mojo:

Gratitude Rant:

Personal Reflections:

159

You know that yahoo who cut you off the other day? How about that snotty woman who you ran into at the store? Those two people, just like all of us, are trying to get through each day. We can accept them for who they are without having them ruin our day.

Actions I Will Take Today to Boost My Mojo:
_____
_____
_____
_____
_____

Gratitude Rant:
_____
_____
_____
_____
_____

Personal Reflections:
_____
_____
_____
_____
_____

160

If you can't change a situation that is unpleasant for you, you have two choices: remove yourself entirely, or graciously accept it and move on. The problem happens when we keep trying to change the unchangeable. It's like banging our heads against a brick wall.

Actions I Will Take Today to Boost My Mojo:

Gratitude Rant:

Personal Reflections:

161

The next time someone does something particularly dim-witted or hurtful, imagine the last time you did something similar. Remember that everyone has weak moments and bad days. Accept it for what it is, and go on enjoying your life.

Actions I Will Take Today to Boost My Mojo:

_____
_____
_____
_____
_____

Gratitude Rant:

_____
_____
_____
_____
_____

Personal Reflections:

_____
_____
_____
_____
_____

162

We are not isolated beings drifting on our own lifeboats. We are all connected through the web of Spirit.

Actions I Will Take Today to Boost My Mojo:

Gratitude Rant:

Personal Reflections:

163

The choices you make affect countless lives each and every day. You can be a powerful agent of change, expansion, and joy if you choose to be.

Actions I Will Take Today to Boost My Mojo:

Gratitude Rant:

Personal Reflections:

164

Imagine a golden strand of energy within you. It extends down to the center of the Earth, high into the Cosmos, and out of your heart toward every other being on the planet. You are a part of a vast system of energy that can support you every step of the way.

Actions I Will Take Today to Boost My Mojo:

___

Gratitude Rant:

___

Personal Reflections:

___

165

Nothing great happens in a vacuum. If you want to create abundance, it starts by reaching out to others in authentic connection. Discover how you can help them. Build supportive, mutually beneficial relationships. Soon you will see that your own dream is being built.

Actions I Will Take Today to Boost My Mojo:

Gratitude Rant:

Personal Reflections:

166

Whenever you are feeling lonely and in need, quiet your mind and make the cosmic phone call to Spirit. Ask for help, and *feel Its presence in your heart.* Sacred connection with Spirit will lift you out of the darkness.

Actions I Will Take Today to Boost My Mojo:

Gratitude Rant:

Personal Reflections:

167

We are often starved of connection, but we also have the cure. Sometimes the best thing we can do is to take a few seconds to look into someone's eyes, acknowledge her presence, and give an appreciative, warm smile. Even better, watch what happens in return.

Actions I Will Take Today to Boost My Mojo:

Gratitude Rant:

Personal Reflections:

YOUR DAILY DOSE OF MOJO

168

To connect with another in a truthful, vulnerable way is one of the most empowering choices you can make. It takes great courage to move out of isolation and into a state of interdependence.

Actions I Will Take Today to Boost My Mojo:

Gratitude Rant:

Personal Reflections:

169

You create every single day. With every choice you create a life. What kind of creation have you made? Drama? Comedy? Horror? Love Story? Which one will you write and star in?

Actions I Will Take Today to Boost My Mojo:
_____
_____
_____
_____
_____

Gratitude Rant:
_____
_____
_____
_____
_____

Personal Reflections:
_____
_____
_____
_____
_____

170

Expressing your creativity is your birthright. It honors the Divine within you.

Actions I Will Take Today to Boost My Mojo:

Gratitude Rant:

Personal Reflections:

171

You are *not too old* to play. Remember what creative activities you used to do as a child? Why don't you take some time today to dust off that notebook, break open the paints, or dance to your favorite song?

Actions I Will Take Today to Boost My Mojo:
_____
_____
_____
_____
_____

Gratitude Rant:
_____
_____
_____
_____
_____

Personal Reflections:
_____
_____
_____
_____
_____

YOUR DAILY DOSE OF MOJO

172

Creativity sparks more creativity. If you are stuck on how to approach an issue, consider letting your artistic, expressive side loose for a while. The energy created will often illuminate other areas in need of clarity.

Actions I Will Take Today to Boost My Mojo:

Gratitude Rant:

Personal Reflections:

173

No one can judge your creations as bad, ugly, or unacceptable. Creativity is a dance of energy between you and Spirit. It is beautiful and perfect.

Actions I Will Take Today to Boost My Mojo:

_____
_____
_____
_____

Gratitude Rant:

_____
_____
_____
_____

Personal Reflections:

_____
_____
_____
_____

174

As you start your day today, imagine how you are going to create it. What wonderful things do you want to have happen? With whom do you want to connect? How do you want to feel? Create your day in your mind first, and let it guide your actions.

Actions I Will Take Today to Boost My Mojo:

Gratitude Rant:

Personal Reflections:

175

It is so satisfying to be an agent of creativity. Let go of the need to execute tasks today, and instead, approach your activities as several acts of creativity. Perform them with a joyful, fresh attitude, and notice how much more you enjoy your day.

Actions I Will Take Today to Boost My Mojo:

Gratitude Rant:

Personal Reflections:

176

Some of our greatest complaints stem from not being heard or acknowledged. Instead of growing resentful, see if you can improve your own listening skills. See others. Hear them. Honor them. You will soon discover that you will be seen, heard, and honored more.

Actions I Will Take Today to Boost My Mojo:

_____
_____
_____
_____
_____

Gratitude Rant:

_____
_____
_____
_____
_____

Personal Reflections:

_____
_____
_____
_____
_____

We communicate not only with our words but also through our actions and inactions. If we have something to say, let's just say it instead of letting our smaller, passive-aggressive side communicate it in a hurtful and unproductive way.

Actions I Will Take Today to Boost My Mojo:

Gratitude Rant:

Personal Reflections:

178

We can't expect people to respond to our requests for help if we don't ever communicate them effectively. We can ask for what we need without whining or feeling weak. It's about choosing our words carefully, being grounded, and staying in our power.

Actions I Will Take Today to Boost My Mojo:

Gratitude Rant:

Personal Reflections:

179

From the wisdom of Dr. Seuss: "Be who you are and say what you mean. Because those who mind don't matter, and those who matter don't mind!" Saying what you mean goes a long way towards simplifying life and lets everyone know where you stand.

Actions I Will Take Today to Boost My Mojo:
_____
_____
_____
_____
_____

Gratitude Rant:
_____
_____
_____
_____
_____

Personal Reflections:
_____
_____
_____
_____
_____

180

If we want love, we will communicate in a loving way. If we want respect, we will communicate respectfully. Conversely, if we communicate in a hurtful, angry way, we will receive that treatment in return. Our communication style dictates our experiences.

Actions I Will Take Today to Boost My Mojo:

Gratitude Rant:

Personal Reflections:

181

Whiny Baby Syndrome is that ugly trap we get into when we let silly things get the better of us. We complain endlessly about how bad things are and then wonder why everything is always so bad. Ditch the whiny baby within, and replace her with your badass superhero.

Actions I Will Take Today to Boost My Mojo:

Gratitude Rant:

Personal Reflections:

182

Most of what we communicate is nonverbal. Watch what other people are really communicating beyond their words and see how you respond. How are you communicating beyond your words? What can you learn that will help you to be more fully understood?

Actions I Will Take Today to Boost My Mojo:

Gratitude Rant:

Personal Reflections:

183

Fear is the biggest enemy you will encounter on your journey toward building your dream. Don't try to get rid of it, but rather get attuned to it, learn from it, and ultimately transform it into power.

Actions I Will Take Today to Boost My Mojo:

Gratitude Rant:

Personal Reflections:

184

Whenever you find yourself in a pickle, ask yourself this question: "What would I do in this situation if I weren't afraid?" And then do that.

Actions I Will Take Today to Boost My Mojo:

Gratitude Rant:

Personal Reflections:

185

Fear is a target that directs you exactly to where you should go. When you boldly go toward your fear and pop it like a balloon, you get to receive the powerful mojo contained within it.

Actions I Will Take Today to Boost My Mojo:

Gratitude Rant:

Personal Reflections:

# 186

It's OK to be afraid. Just don't let that be where you stop. See it on your path, stop to visit it, learn from it, and then keep going, allowing it to fade away in your rearview mirror.

Actions I Will Take Today to Boost My Mojo:

Gratitude Rant:

Personal Reflections:

187

Fear should be perceived as an acute, temporary response to a potential threat. It will pass, and you will return to your normal, powerful self. Don't let fear become the chronic condition that keeps you bedridden for life.

Actions I Will Take Today to Boost My Mojo:

Gratitude Rant:

Personal Reflections:

188

Learn to make relations with fear. Recognize it in yourself. Smell it. Fear is a container that holds a tremendous amount of potential energy. We can either let it guide us, or we can use it to our advantage on our quest for Bigness.

Actions I Will Take Today to Boost My Mojo:

Gratitude Rant:

Personal Reflections:

189

Fear is like a cheap perfume that makes us look bad, stinks up our environment, and ruins our chances to get lucky. Power, on the other hand, is a potent attractor of all that you desire. You deserve *the good stuff*.

Actions I Will Take Today to Boost My Mojo:
_____
_____
_____
_____
_____

Gratitude Rant:
_____
_____
_____
_____
_____

Personal Reflections:
_____
_____
_____
_____
_____

190

I believe in the Boomerang Theory: what we send out returns to us in kind. Remember the boomerang today, and make sure you are tossing only good things out into the world.

Actions I Will Take Today to Boost My Mojo:

Gratitude Rant:

Personal Reflections:

191

When we consciously make our choices with the knowing that they will return to us in a similar way, it cleans up our actions and keeps us in alignment with the highest good of all.

Actions I Will Take Today to Boost My Mojo:

Gratitude Rant:

Personal Reflections:

192

If you are struggling financially, don't keep obsessing about how little money you have. Instead, attract more of the green energy to you by sharing some with others, being grateful for what you do have, and inviting more of it into your life.

Actions I Will Take Today to Boost My Mojo:

_____
_____
_____
_____
_____

Gratitude Rant:

_____
_____
_____
_____
_____

Personal Reflections:

_____
_____
_____
_____
_____

193

Be a magnet of joy.

Actions I Will Take Today to Boost My Mojo:

Gratitude Rant:

Personal Reflections:

194

You cannot stop energy. Things are going to come at you whether you like it or not. Given that you receive what you send out, what kind of energy do you want to transmit?
What do you want to attract?

Actions I Will Take Today to Boost My Mojo:

Gratitude Rant:

Personal Reflections:

195

When we fill our heads with negative self-talk, we are also sending that energy out into the world. As a result, we attract situations and people that validate what we sent out. Say only good things about yourself so others will do the same.

Actions I Will Take Today to Boost My Mojo:

Gratitude Rant:

Personal Reflections:

196

If you are clear in what you want and humbly communicate it on a regular basis, you will naturally attract those people, circumstances, and opportunities that will help you realize your dreams. People want to help you.

Actions I Will Take Today to Boost My Mojo:

Gratitude Rant:

Personal Reflections:

Making time an adversary is a recipe for pain. Time will always be a presence in your life, so it is in your best interest to consciously interact with it.
Make it a friend.

Actions I Will Take Today to Boost My Mojo:

Gratitude Rant:

Personal Reflections:

198

We each have the same amount of time to spend. We have 1440 minutes to spend every day in whatever way we choose. Make each minute count. At least, don't give away too much of your precious resource to mindless TV.

Actions I Will Take Today to Boost My Mojo:

Gratitude Rant:

Personal Reflections:

199

Decide what activities you want to do today and what is realistic. Figure out exactly what time you are going to get them done. Put them in your calendar, and honor the commitment to yourself. Even if you put in only two or three things, your productivity will skyrocket.

Actions I Will Take Today to Boost My Mojo:
_____
_____
_____
_____
_____

Gratitude Rant:
_____
_____
_____
_____
_____

Personal Reflections:
_____
_____
_____
_____
_____

200

Reclaim your time, and let your calendar be your servant, not your master. You, no one else, get to choose how you spend your time. By claiming ownership of your time, you are claiming ownership of your life.

Actions I Will Take Today to Boost My Mojo:

Gratitude Rant:

Personal Reflections:

201

One of my favorite quotes is from Annie Dillard: "How we spend our days is, of course, how we spend our lives." Don't get too caught up in the everyday noise of tasks and to-dos, forgetting that you are, in fact, living your life.

Actions I Will Take Today to Boost My Mojo:

Gratitude Rant:

Personal Reflections:

202

Life is finite, and there will be a moment in the future when you will literally run out of time. But you aren't there yet. There is nothing you can't pursue because you don't have time. You have all of the time in the world; you just need to spend it mindfully.

Actions I Will Take Today to Boost My Mojo:
_____
_____
_____
_____
_____

Gratitude Rant:
_____
_____
_____
_____
_____

Personal Reflections:
_____
_____
_____
_____
_____

203

The time you dedicate toward the realization of your dream is time well spent. Don't be stingy with yourself and give all of your time away to others. Your dream needs care and feeding; it won't grow without you giving some time to it.

Actions I Will Take Today to Boost My Mojo:

Gratitude Rant:

Personal Reflections:

204

Our words contain energy and intention. By choosing our words carefully, we design our lives instead of living them by default.

Actions I Will Take Today to Boost My Mojo:

Gratitude Rant:

Personal Reflections:

205

Words can harm or they can heal.
They can create or destroy.
They can energize or demoralize.
They are powerful instruments of
transformation or destruction.
Let your words be filled with Light.

Actions I Will Take Today to Boost My Mojo:

Gratitude Rant:

Personal Reflections:

YOUR DAILY DOSE OF MOJO

206

Don't use negative words to describe yourself. Reframe your "negative" traits into words of empowerment. Be curvaceous! Be wise! Be seasoned! Be colorful! Be you.

Actions I Will Take Today to Boost My Mojo:

_____
_____
_____
_____
_____

Gratitude Rant:

_____
_____
_____
_____
_____

Personal Reflections:

_____
_____
_____
_____
_____

Try to banish the phrase "have to" from your vocabulary. You don't *have to* do anything; you *get to* do them. Conscious use of language can transform your life.

Actions I Will Take Today to Boost My Mojo:

Gratitude Rant:

Personal Reflections:

208

Notice how many negative words you use in a day. How many times do you say, "can't," "couldn't," "shouldn't," or "won't"? Consider "positivizing" your words—you can, you could, you should, and you WILL!
See how much better those feel?

Actions I Will Take Today to Boost My Mojo:

Gratitude Rant:

Personal Reflections:

209

Write out your dream in a nutshell and make it exactly what you want in your life. When it is perfect, say it out loud. Did you stumble over any of your desires, or have a lump in your throat? Keep reciting the dream until you actually believe it.

Actions I Will Take Today to Boost My Mojo:

Gratitude Rant:

Personal Reflections:

210

Do not accept sloppy language in yourself or others. Gently but firmly hold everyone accountable to speak from a place of truth, integrity, and compassion.

Actions I Will Take Today to Boost My Mojo:

Gratitude Rant:

Personal Reflections:

211

To forgive is to be free.

Actions I Will Take Today to Boost My Mojo:

Gratitude Rant:

Personal Reflections:

212

Last time I checked, no manual exists on How to Be a Perfect Person. We all do the best we can, and sometimes we fall short. It is at those times when we can show compassion and forgiveness instead of donning our Judgment Hat.

Actions I Will Take Today to Boost My Mojo:

Gratitude Rant:

Personal Reflections:

213

Write a sticky note that says, "Who Can I Forgive Today?" and place it somewhere you'll see it frequently. (Mine is on the bathroom mirror.) You are guaranteed to spend at least a little bit of time in your heart every single day.

Actions I Will Take Today to Boost My Mojo:

Gratitude Rant:

Personal Reflections:

214

Forgiveness isn't weak, nor does it excuse bad behavior. It frees one's mind of the toxicity of resentment and enables forward momentum.

Actions I Will Take Today to Boost My Mojo:

Gratitude Rant:

Personal Reflections:

215

Forgiveness allows us to deepen our awareness of the unity of all things. By looking at another's poor choices and forgiving them, it gives us an opportunity to see where we have fallen short and release ourselves from lurking guilt.

Actions I Will Take Today to Boost My Mojo:

Gratitude Rant:

Personal Reflections:

YOUR DAILY DOSE OF MOJO

216

You grow your personal power every time you let go of anger and blame. The more you forgive, the bigger you get.

Actions I Will Take Today to Boost My Mojo:

Gratitude Rant:

Personal Reflections:

217

Forgiveness is the antidote to judgment and shame.

Actions I Will Take Today to Boost My Mojo:

Gratitude Rant:

Personal Reflections:

218

Your future is first determined in your head. You see your new reality in your mind's eye and then the physical world begins to carve itself around your vision.

Actions I Will Take Today to Boost My Mojo:

Gratitude Rant:

Personal Reflections:

219

If you can't see your dream, you can't realize it.

Actions I Will Take Today to Boost My Mojo:

Gratitude Rant:

Personal Reflections:

220

Allow yourself some sacred time to visualize your ideal life. See every aspect in rich Technicolor. Immerse yourself in it. Step into the new skin of the Bigger You. See it. Feel it. KNOW it.

Actions I Will Take Today to Boost My Mojo:
___
___
___
___
___

Gratitude Rant:
___
___
___
___
___

Personal Reflections:
___
___
___
___
___

221

The next time you find yourself in a conflict or another difficult situation, imagine the most positive outcome. See peaceful resolution. Jump to the good part. Your vision will help bring it about.

Actions I Will Take Today to Boost My Mojo:
_____
_____
_____
_____
_____

Gratitude Rant:
_____
_____
_____
_____
_____

Personal Reflections:
_____
_____
_____
_____

YOUR DAILY DOSE OF MOJO

222

Envisioning failure is dripping poison on your dream's seeds. Instead, water them frequently with visions of joy, balance and success.

Actions I Will Take Today to Boost My Mojo:

Gratitude Rant:

Personal Reflections:

223

Just as Michael Jordan visualized the ball going into the hoop when standing at the free throw line, so too can you visualize the successful outcome of your endeavors. Swish!

Actions I Will Take Today to Boost My Mojo:
___
___
___
___
___

Gratitude Rant:
___
___
___
___
___

Personal Reflections:
___
___
___
___
___

224

A well-defined vision is the blueprint of your dream. Give Spirit clear instructions by creating a powerful, abundant vision of your future.

Actions I Will Take Today to Boost My Mojo:

Gratitude Rant:

Personal Reflections:

225

Your relationship with finances is yours. Don't let the money stories of your parents or other influencers become your baggage to tote around.

Actions I Will Take Today to Boost My Mojo:
_____
_____
_____
_____
_____

Gratitude Rant:
_____
_____
_____
_____
_____

Personal Reflections:
_____
_____
_____
_____
_____

226

Money is not negative or positive. It doesn't play favorites. It is neutral. It is an energy. Therefore, you can decide how you want to interact with it. Do you want it to be a positive, abundant source, or one that is negative and scarce?

Actions I Will Take Today to Boost My Mojo:

___

Gratitude Rant:

___

Personal Reflections:

___

227

The next time you purchase something, take a moment to appreciate the energy you gave to bring that money into your life. Be grateful for the chance to have earned the money so you could enjoy your new item. Your mindfulness and gratitude will bring more of it to you.

Actions I Will Take Today to Boost My Mojo:

Gratitude Rant:

Personal Reflections:

228

Visualize a steady stream of money energy flowing toward you and around you. Interact with it naturally and playfully. Imagine fun ways it will enter your life. You never know what sort of magic your visualization will kick off.

Actions I Will Take Today to Boost My Mojo:

Gratitude Rant:

Personal Reflections:

229

Money isn't a bad thing. It is something we use to support our needs, help serve others, and create space for joy. When we respect it without idolizing it, money can be a catalyst for good.

Actions I Will Take Today to Boost My Mojo:

_____
_____
_____
_____
_____

Gratitude Rant:

_____
_____
_____
_____
_____

Personal Reflections:

_____
_____
_____
_____
_____

230

Even when you are in the throes of major financial woes, you can still find ways to show gratitude for what you do have. Focus on your blessings instead of what you lack. Your gratitude will get you through until the wave of green comes your way.

Actions I Will Take Today to Boost My Mojo:

_____
_____
_____
_____
_____

Gratitude Rant:

_____
_____
_____
_____
_____

Personal Reflections:

_____
_____
_____
_____
_____

231

You deserve to be financially secure.

Actions I Will Take Today to Boost My Mojo:

Gratitude Rant:

Personal Reflections:

232

Resisting change is like holding your breath. It's ultimately pointless and just makes you feel sick. Breathe deeply and easily into change.

Actions I Will Take Today to Boost My Mojo:

Gratitude Rant:

Personal Reflections:

233

Perceive change as a flow of energy that
is transporting you
to a fabulous new reality.

Actions I Will Take Today to Boost My Mojo:
_____
_____
_____
_____
_____

Gratitude Rant:
_____
_____
_____
_____
_____

Personal Reflections:
_____
_____
_____
_____
_____

234

Going through great change can create a tendency for us to become paralyzed by fear. Combat this paralysis by moving your body more. The joy will unlock hidden strength within you that will help you confidently move to the next phase.

Actions I Will Take Today to Boost My Mojo:

_____
_____
_____
_____
_____

Gratitude Rant:

_____
_____
_____
_____
_____

Personal Reflections:

_____
_____
_____
_____
_____

235

"This too shall pass" was one of my mother's favorite sayings. It is a potent reminder that all things are temporary, so we needn't attach ourselves too strongly to them. Let yourself flow through the change.

Actions I Will Take Today to Boost My Mojo:

Gratitude Rant:

Personal Reflections:

236

Nature functions in cycles, and we are a part of nature. Sometimes we are in the newness of Spring, the bustling activity of Summer, the abundant harvest of Autumn, or the quiet stillness of Winter. Sometimes we bloom, and sometimes we hibernate. Embracing the cycle of change helps us to live more fully.

Actions I Will Take Today to Boost My Mojo:

Gratitude Rant:

Personal Reflections:

237

Sometimes you can change your circumstances, and sometimes they are beyond your physical control. However, you always have the capacity to change your perspective. Your ability to choose joy over victimhood can counteract any unpleasantness.

Actions I Will Take Today to Boost My Mojo:

Gratitude Rant:

Personal Reflections:

238

A mother can't stop the process of labor and birth. It can be an incredibly painful process, but it is necessary and will eventually be over. Relaxing and breathing through change will help you birth your future as smoothly as possible. The pain will eventually pass.

Actions I Will Take Today to Boost My Mojo:

Gratitude Rant:

Personal Reflections:

239

We cannot avoid loss, but we can choose to make it a sacred, transformational moment.

Actions I Will Take Today to Boost My Mojo:
___
___
___
___
___

Gratitude Rant:
___
___
___
___
___

Personal Reflections:
___
___
___
___
___

240

Whenever the pain of loss feels too great, remember the wisdom of Dr. Seuss: "Don't cry because it's over. Smile because it happened."

Actions I Will Take Today to Boost My Mojo:

Gratitude Rant:

Personal Reflections:

241

The tears we shed for those who have transitioned to the Spirit World are physical reminders of
the love in our hearts.

Actions I Will Take Today to Boost My Mojo:

Gratitude Rant:

Personal Reflections:

242

Don't run away from the intensity of grief. Feel it to your core. Allow yourself to scream like an Italian grandmother at a funeral. You will emerge on the other side both healthier and stronger than ever before.

Actions I Will Take Today to Boost My Mojo:

_____
_____
_____
_____
_____

Gratitude Rant:

_____
_____
_____
_____
_____

Personal Reflections:

_____
_____
_____
_____
_____

243

Unprocessed grief will act as an anchor, keeping you firmly embedded in a quiet state of sorrow and loss. Ask for help, feel the pain fully, and release it to Spirit for transformation. You will find that the light shines a little brighter after having let the anchor go.

Actions I Will Take Today to Boost My Mojo:

Gratitude Rant:

Personal Reflections:

244

We can grieve over more than just the death of a loved one. We can grieve the loss of a relationship, a home, an identity, or anything else that deeply defined us. Allow yourself to honor your loss, and give yourself permission to be a bit tender in the healing process.

Actions I Will Take Today to Boost My Mojo:

Gratitude Rant:

Personal Reflections:

245

Take a moment to connect with the spirit of someone special to you who is no longer in physical form. Remember how his or her hands felt. Recall one of your favorite memories. Let your heart fill with joy and appreciation. Make it a sacred energetic interaction. Profound grief can accompany deep gratitude.

Actions I Will Take Today to Boost My Mojo:

Gratitude Rant:

Personal Reflections:

YOUR DAILY DOSE OF MOJO

246

A never-ending flow of energy is circulating the Universe. That flow is tapped into you and is available at any time.

Actions I Will Take Today to Boost My Mojo:

Gratitude Rant:

Personal Reflections:

247

Allow, accept, and embrace all that Spirit has in store for you.

Actions I Will Take Today to Boost My Mojo:

Gratitude Rant:

Personal Reflections:

YOUR DAILY DOSE OF MOJO

248

Taking a gratitude bath reminds us that we are already rich beyond measure.

Actions I Will Take Today to Boost My Mojo:

_____
_____
_____
_____
_____

Gratitude Rant:

_____
_____
_____
_____
_____

Personal Reflections:

_____
_____
_____
_____
_____

249

You are enough—
and you have enough.

Actions I Will Take Today to Boost My Mojo:

Gratitude Rant:

Personal Reflections:

250

The Bigger You is abundant in all areas. The Bigger You knows that the key lies in joyful living, mindfulness, an open heart, and a connection to Spirit.

Actions I Will Take Today to Boost My Mojo:

Gratitude Rant:

Personal Reflections:

251

It's exhausting to continually chase after what might have been or what could be. A truly abundant person is fully satisfied with what is.

Actions I Will Take Today to Boost My Mojo:

Gratitude Rant:

Personal Reflections:

252

Feel abundant, and you will become abundant. Feel a sense of lack, and you will experience it. Everything starts with a feeling.

Actions I Will Take Today to Boost My Mojo:

_____
_____
_____
_____
_____

Gratitude Rant:

_____
_____
_____
_____
_____

Personal Reflections:

_____
_____
_____
_____
_____

253

Everyone has a reason for being. What is your purpose, and how does it serve humanity? Don't ever minimize your impact. Your presence is a part of Spirit's plan.

Actions I Will Take Today to Boost My Mojo:

_____
_____
_____
_____
_____

Gratitude Rant:

_____
_____
_____
_____
_____

Personal Reflections:

_____
_____
_____
_____
_____

254

Create a daily intention. What is your purpose every day? If you define your purpose, you are more apt to fulfill it.

Actions I Will Take Today to Boost My Mojo:

Gratitude Rant:

Personal Reflections:

255

Your life's purpose is your rudder. It will guide you through all of the rough waters of challenge, keeping you focused on where you want to go.

Actions I Will Take Today to Boost My Mojo:

Gratitude Rant:

Personal Reflections:

256

If we understand WHY we are doing something, we are far more likely to continue to take action towards its success.

Actions I Will Take Today to Boost My Mojo:

Gratitude Rant:

Personal Reflections:

257

A dream without a purpose is just a fantasy.

Actions I Will Take Today to Boost My Mojo:

Gratitude Rant:

Personal Reflections:

YOUR DAILY DOSE OF MOJO

258

Purpose puts meaning in our pursuits. It brings with it the energy of service that always acts a catalyst for manifestation.

Actions I Will Take Today to Boost My Mojo:

___

Gratitude Rant:

___

Personal Reflections:

___

259

Your abundance and well-being are directly tied to your life's purpose. The Universe rewards those who make it count.

Actions I Will Take Today to Boost My Mojo:

_____
_____
_____
_____
_____

Gratitude Rant:

_____
_____
_____
_____
_____

Personal Reflections:

_____
_____
_____
_____
_____

260

By living mindfully, we create a more fulfilling life while contributing to the well-being of our communities.

Actions I Will Take Today to Boost My Mojo:

Gratitude Rant:

Personal Reflections:

261

Consciously choose the food you eat.
Make meals that are good for you while
being good for the planet.
What you take in has a bearing on
what you send out.

Actions I Will Take Today to Boost My Mojo:

_____
_____
_____
_____
_____

Gratitude Rant:

_____
_____
_____
_____
_____

Personal Reflections:

_____
_____
_____
_____
_____

YOUR DAILY DOSE OF MOJO

262

Remember when you were taught as a kid to pick up after yourself? Now that we are adults, we make bigger environmental messes. It's our responsibility to clean them up.

Actions I Will Take Today to Boost My Mojo:

Gratitude Rant:

Personal Reflections:

263

Don't you HATE it when people yak away in the movie theatre? It's an obnoxious display of unconsciousness and affects everyone around them. By being mindful of others, we strengthen our community and promote goodwill. Identify ways you can make a positive contribution.

Actions I Will Take Today to Boost My Mojo:

Gratitude Rant:

Personal Reflections:

264

With awareness comes consciousness.
When we truly notice the world around
us and our role in it,
we can make conscious choices
to be a force for good.

Actions I Will Take Today to Boost My Mojo:

Gratitude Rant:

Personal Reflections:

265

Be aware of your physical, mental, emotional, and spiritual needs. Recognize that all of these aspects are interconnected, and your wellness depends on caring for every facet.

Actions I Will Take Today to Boost My Mojo:
_____
_____
_____
_____
_____

Gratitude Rant:
_____
_____
_____
_____
_____

Personal Reflections:
_____
_____
_____
_____
_____

266

Any camper will tell you that you are instructed to "leave no trace" of your presence in nature. If it's good enough for the campground, then it is good enough for our *lifeground*. Let's walk lightly and leave our little patch of land better than we found it.

Actions I Will Take Today to Boost My Mojo:

Gratitude Rant:

Personal Reflections:

267

A path that is paved with service is a path to peace and prosperity.

Actions I Will Take Today to Boost My Mojo:

_____
_____
_____
_____
_____

Gratitude Rant:

_____
_____
_____
_____
_____

Personal Reflections:

_____
_____
_____
_____
_____

268

Adopting a service-oriented approach to business will have more of an impact on your bottom line than any other strategy, product, or program you could utilize.

Actions I Will Take Today to Boost My Mojo:

Gratitude Rant:

Personal Reflections:

269

Stepping out of our personal dramas and into service of others in need can transform our dark moments into Divine ones.

Actions I Will Take Today to Boost My Mojo:

_____
_____
_____
_____
_____

Gratitude Rant:

_____
_____
_____
_____
_____

Personal Reflections:

_____
_____
_____
_____
_____

YOUR DAILY DOSE OF MOJO

270

The best way to engage in a new relationship with a colleague is to ask yourself, "How can I help?" By genuinely valuing the needs of others in addition to your own, you will get noticed and earn respect.

Actions I Will Take Today to Boost My Mojo:

Gratitude Rant:

Personal Reflections:

271

Mahatma Gandhi said, "The best way to find yourself is to lose yourself in the service of others." If you are at a crossroads or in a place of uncertainty, consider taking the focus off you and onto others. You will gain clarity through the act of service.

Actions I Will Take Today to Boost My Mojo:

Gratitude Rant:

Personal Reflections:

272

A life of service doesn't have to look like Mother Teresa's work. You can be a significant force of good by incorporating simple acts of giving throughout your day.

Actions I Will Take Today to Boost My Mojo:

Gratitude Rant:

Personal Reflections:

273

As you start your day, ask yourself how you can best serve today. Who needs your help? What light can you bring to a dark situation? What gift can you give that brings joy and comfort to another?

Actions I Will Take Today to Boost My Mojo:

Gratitude Rant:

Personal Reflections:

YOUR DAILY DOSE OF MOJO

274

It is never, ever, ever too late to transform yourself into the Bigger You.

Actions I Will Take Today to Boost My Mojo:

Gratitude Rant:

Personal Reflections:

275

Just as water can go from a solid form to a liquid or gas, you too can transform into a new state of being if you choose. All it takes is intention, action, and time.

Actions I Will Take Today to Boost My Mojo:

_____
_____
_____
_____

Gratitude Rant:

_____
_____
_____
_____
_____

Personal Reflections:

_____
_____
_____
_____
_____

276

There isn't a point where you will declare, "I am transformed!" It is a gradual process that happens over time. Someday, however, you will recognize that your life isn't anything like it used to be.

Actions I Will Take Today to Boost My Mojo:

Gratitude Rant:

Personal Reflections:

277

Transformation occurs somewhere on the path of a thousand conscious choices.

Actions I Will Take Today to Boost My Mojo:

Gratitude Rant:

Personal Reflections:

278

Clark Kent doesn't transform into Superman. He already IS Superman; he merely takes off the glasses and dons the tights. We are also superheroes—we just need to start wearing it more often.

Actions I Will Take Today to Boost My Mojo:

Gratitude Rant:

Personal Reflections:

279

We can transform any negative situation into a positive one through simple, but not always easy, acts of gratitude and forgiveness.

Actions I Will Take Today to Boost My Mojo:

Gratitude Rant:

Personal Reflections:

YOUR DAILY DOSE OF MOJO

280

Growth and transformation aren't always comfortable. The caterpillar wasn't having a blast in the chrysalis, but the effort was worth it. You will have your days of discomfort. Trust that it is a natural part of your process.

Actions I Will Take Today to Boost My Mojo:

___

Gratitude Rant:

___

Personal Reflections:

___

# 281

Regularly moving your body in joy will give you the energy you need to create the life you desire.

Actions I Will Take Today to Boost My Mojo:
_____
_____
_____
_____

Gratitude Rant:
_____
_____
_____
_____

Personal Reflections:
_____
_____
_____
_____

282

If we live a sedentary lifestyle, we are cutting off a significant source of power available to us. Oxygenating the blood, moving the muscles, and getting out of our heads, all have tremendous value in helping us to create our dreams.

Actions I Will Take Today to Boost My Mojo:

_____
_____
_____
_____
_____

Gratitude Rant:

_____
_____
_____
_____
_____

Personal Reflections:

_____
_____
_____
_____
_____

283

Don't worry about moving your body the way others do it. Just find something that feels good to you. Discover the activity that you genuinely love. Your love will give you the discipline to do it regularly.

Actions I Will Take Today to Boost My Mojo:
_____
_____
_____
_____
_____

Gratitude Rant:
_____
_____
_____
_____
_____

Personal Reflections:
_____
_____
_____
_____
_____

284

Exercise is horrible. The word itself is rife with obligation, negativity, and judgment. I hope you never exercise another day in your life. But you absolutely, positively have permission to play.

Actions I Will Take Today to Boost My Mojo:

Gratitude Rant:

Personal Reflections:

285

Moving in joy has no rules. There aren't target heart rates, optimal durations, or sets of reps. It's simple. Just move your body in a way that feels good, stop when you are done, and do it again tomorrow.

Actions I Will Take Today to Boost My Mojo:

Gratitude Rant:

Personal Reflections:

286

When we move our bodies with the intention of infusing them with joy and removing all stress and worry, our practice becomes more than physical; it become a moving meditation.

Actions I Will Take Today to Boost My Mojo:

Gratitude Rant:

Personal Reflections:

287

When we move physically, we also move mentally into greater empowerment, emotionally into deeper compassion, and spiritually into higher consciousness.

Actions I Will Take Today to Boost My Mojo:

Gratitude Rant:

Personal Reflections:

288

You have a network of support that wants to help you attain your dreams. You may not know all of the members yet, but they are on their way to you.

Actions I Will Take Today to Boost My Mojo:

Gratitude Rant:

Personal Reflections:

289

If you don't know how to do something that is important in the realization of your dreams, then ask Spirit to point you in the right direction. Ask for the right teachings to present themselves. Be open to the lessons that are available to you.

Actions I Will Take Today to Boost My Mojo:

Gratitude Rant:

Personal Reflections:

290

My mother's favorite inspirational book was *Think and Grow Rich* by Napoleon Hill. It is a profound resource for expansion that describes how the things we can conceive and believe, we can also achieve.
If you haven't read it, check it out!

Actions I Will Take Today to Boost My Mojo:

Gratitude Rant:

Personal Reflections:

291

Those that support you and your dream are allies. Those that do not are saboteurs. Make sure your orbit contains only allies, or at the very least, put the saboteurs on mute.

Actions I Will Take Today to Boost My Mojo:
_____
_____
_____
_____
_____

Gratitude Rant:
_____
_____
_____
_____
_____

Personal Reflections:
_____
_____
_____
_____
_____

292

Books, recordings, classes, workshops, seminars, coaching, and training programs are available to help you realize your dreams. Resources abound. All you need to do is tune into the right ones for you and then take action.

Actions I Will Take Today to Boost My Mojo:

Gratitude Rant:

Personal Reflections:

293

Endless resources are available on the Internet. However, be careful that your screen time doesn't become a distraction. It's easy to lose yourself to your computer.
Remember, real life happens when the power buttons are off.

Actions I Will Take Today to Boost My Mojo:

Gratitude Rant:

Personal Reflections:

294

Your list of allies will grow when you become an advocate for others. People want to help those who help others. Who can you help today?

Actions I Will Take Today to Boost My Mojo:

Gratitude Rant:

Personal Reflections:

295

Cultivating awareness helps you to see the landscape of your life more clearly so you can make the best possible choices.

Actions I Will Take Today to Boost My Mojo:

Gratitude Rant:

Personal Reflections:

296

You can't make physical changes to your health until you really know yourself. How does your body feel? What do you think it needs to feel better? What steps can you take to improve your health and well-being?

Actions I Will Take Today to Boost My Mojo:

_____
_____
_____
_____
_____

Gratitude Rant:

_____
_____
_____
_____
_____

Personal Reflections:

_____
_____
_____
_____
_____

297

We spend so much of our time on computers, smartphones, and tablets. It's important to make the effort to look up every once in a while. When we are aware of our surroundings, we become more present in the moment.

Actions I Will Take Today to Boost My Mojo:

Gratitude Rant:

Personal Reflections:

298

Becoming more aware of ourselves, our environment and those around us does not involve judgment. It is simply observing what is, not what should be. By knowing what is really going on—good or bad—you can make informed decisions.

Actions I Will Take Today to Boost My Mojo:

_____
_____
_____
_____
_____

Gratitude Rant:

_____
_____
_____
_____
_____

Personal Reflections:

_____
_____
_____
_____
_____

299

Sometimes we don't even know how sad, angry, or depressed we are because we are so busy on the hamster wheel of to-dos and tasks. Do regular internal check-ins on how you feel. Become mindful of your emotional state. Once you know where you are, you can decide where you want to be.

Actions I Will Take Today to Boost My Mojo:

_____
_____
_____
_____
_____

Gratitude Rant:

_____
_____
_____
_____
_____

Personal Reflections:

_____
_____
_____
_____

YOUR DAILY DOSE OF MOJO

300

When you are called to serve based on a keen awareness of a genuine need and how you can best contribute, the act of service becomes a sacred one.

Actions I Will Take Today to Boost My Mojo:

Gratitude Rant:

Personal Reflections:

301

Those who are awake, aware, and alert to the signs from the Universe are those who are living freely and fully.

Actions I Will Take Today to Boost My Mojo:

_____
_____
_____
_____
_____

Gratitude Rant:

_____
_____
_____
_____
_____

Personal Reflections:

_____
_____
_____
_____
_____

302

You already know how to do what it takes to realize your dream. The trick is to be open to the nonphysical presence of Spirit so you can follow the guidance given to you.

Actions I Will Take Today to Boost My Mojo:

Gratitude Rant:

Personal Reflections:

303

Ask the right questions and wait for the answers to present themselves. Trust in your gut feelings and the signs placed before you.

Actions I Will Take Today to Boost My Mojo:

Gratitude Rant:

Personal Reflections:

304

What does your body feel like when it senses a "Yes" or a "No"? By training yourself to use your physical body as a recipient of intuition, you gain access to the most powerful form of assistance, the Divine Guidance System (DGS).

Actions I Will Take Today to Boost My Mojo:
_____
_____
_____
_____
_____

Gratitude Rant:
_____
_____
_____
_____
_____

Personal Reflections:
_____
_____
_____
_____
_____

305

Your intuition can be a powerful compass when you are lost in the mire of your story.

Actions I Will Take Today to Boost My Mojo:
_____
_____
_____
_____
_____

Gratitude Rant:
_____
_____
_____
_____
_____

Personal Reflections:
_____
_____
_____
_____
_____

306

Having a keen intuition comes from being consistently tuned into the messages and nuances that Spirit is sending you through vision, sensation, dreams, synchronicity. and other forms of connection.

Actions I Will Take Today to Boost My Mojo:

Gratitude Rant:

Personal Reflections:

307

Trusting in the power of your intuition allows you to have a spirit advisor with you at all times, helping you to navigate difficult terrain. You don't have to know it all; you can rely on the sacred guidance you receive.

Actions I Will Take Today to Boost My Mojo:

Gratitude Rant:

Personal Reflections:

308

Your task isn't to figure out how to go after your dreams—it's listening to and acting upon the Divine guidance that leads the journey.

Actions I Will Take Today to Boost My Mojo:

Gratitude Rant:

Personal Reflections:

309

You are a person of abundance who shares many gifts and talents with the world, whether they are acknowledged or not.

Actions I Will Take Today to Boost My Mojo:
_____
_____
_____
_____
_____

Gratitude Rant:
_____
_____
_____
_____
_____

Personal Reflections:
_____
_____
_____
_____
_____

310

Reflect on your skills and talents as a child. What were you particularly gifted at doing? Recall the joy you felt. What you could bring into your life that would elicit that same joyful response?

Actions I Will Take Today to Boost My Mojo:

Gratitude Rant:

Personal Reflections:

311

We are meant to share our creative gifts with the world. It is a caring, bold act to share ourselves with others. It is a gift of grace and courage.

Actions I Will Take Today to Boost My Mojo:

Gratitude Rant:

Personal Reflections:

312

Unapologetically *declare your magnificence.* You can appreciate the many gifts and talents you possess without feeling ashamed or unworthy.

Actions I Will Take Today to Boost My Mojo:

Gratitude Rant:

Personal Reflections:

313

We often focus too strongly on our negative aspects instead of celebrating our positive ones. Make a mental list of some of the many gifts you bring to the world. You give to so many, and on behalf of everyone in your orbit, we thank you.

Actions I Will Take Today to Boost My Mojo:

Gratitude Rant:

Personal Reflections:

YOUR DAILY DOSE OF MOJO

314

Our talents don't have to possess economic value. They can simply be the precious pearls we lovingly share, all for the sake of joy.

Actions I Will Take Today to Boost My Mojo:

Gratitude Rant:

Personal Reflections:

315

Never shy away from a moment of genuine appreciation for your many gifts. When someone compliments you or recognizes your efforts, graciously accept it and say thank you. You've earned it.

Actions I Will Take Today to Boost My Mojo:

Gratitude Rant:

Personal Reflections:

316

Doors of opportunity surround you. All you need to do is go through the door that your intuition
is nudging you towards.

Actions I Will Take Today to Boost My Mojo:

Gratitude Rant:

Personal Reflections:

317

If it is truly a great opportunity, then there should be at least a little fear or risk involved. If not, then it isn't that big of a deal. There's always an emotional charge when something amazing is just around the corner.

Actions I Will Take Today to Boost My Mojo:
_____
_____
_____
_____
_____

Gratitude Rant:
_____
_____
_____
_____
_____

Personal Reflections:
_____
_____
_____
_____
_____

YOUR DAILY DOSE OF MOJO

318

If we perceive every new endeavor as an opportunity to learn and grow, regardless if it is a success or failure, then we step out of our bubble of safety and actually start living fully.

Actions I Will Take Today to Boost My Mojo:

Gratitude Rant:

Personal Reflections:

319

Spirit presents us with opportunities to further our dream all of the time. They can come the form of intuitive hits, coincidences, or chance meetings. Follow the nudge, and *see where it takes you.*

Actions I Will Take Today to Boost My Mojo:
_____
_____
_____
_____
_____

Gratitude Rant:
_____
_____
_____
_____
_____

Personal Reflections:
_____
_____
_____
_____
_____

… YOUR DAILY DOSE OF MOJO

320

Every moment is an opportunity to choose. Even when you are stuck in traffic on the way to a big event, you still have the opportunity
to choose how you will react.

Actions I Will Take Today to Boost My Mojo:

_____
_____
_____
_____
_____

Gratitude Rant:

_____
_____
_____
_____
_____

Personal Reflections:

_____
_____
_____
_____
_____

321

Attitude affects opportunity. The healthier and more powerful you feel, the greater the likelihood that yummy opportunities will present themselves to you.

Actions I Will Take Today to Boost My Mojo:
_____
_____
_____
_____
_____

Gratitude Rant:
_____
_____
_____
_____
_____

Personal Reflections:
_____
_____
_____
_____
_____

322

Opportunities sprout in the fields of your passion, belief, and dedication.

Actions I Will Take Today to Boost My Mojo:

Gratitude Rant:

Personal Reflections:

323

You possess the ultimate freedom: the freedom to choose. You get to choose the person you want to be, and the life you want to live. Your choice holds your independence.

Actions I Will Take Today to Boost My Mojo:

_____
_____
_____
_____
_____

Gratitude Rant:

_____
_____
_____
_____
_____

Personal Reflections:

_____
_____
_____
_____
_____

324

We can be free of our dramas, our old wounds, and our boo-hoo stories whenever we choose. They no longer need to haunt us once we simply decide to forgive and let go.

Actions I Will Take Today to Boost My Mojo:

Gratitude Rant:

Personal Reflections:

325

We are free to love whomever and live however we choose, and others are free to have an opinion about our choices. However, one doesn't affect the other.

Actions I Will Take Today to Boost My Mojo:

Gratitude Rant:

Personal Reflections:

326

Sometimes we convince ourselves that we have no free will. We often create scenarios that feel as if we have no control over them. We tell ourselves that we "have to" do something. In reality, we choose our lives by exercising our free will.

Actions I Will Take Today to Boost My Mojo:

Gratitude Rant:

Personal Reflections:

327

Don't see time off from work as "free" time. Given that most of us work half of our waking lives, shouldn't we start approaching work with as much joy as our time off? Why settle for being happy 50 percent of the time when you can be 100 percent?

Actions I Will Take Today to Boost My Mojo:
_____
_____
_____
_____
_____

Gratitude Rant:
_____
_____
_____
_____
_____

Personal Reflections:
_____
_____
_____
_____
_____

328

Just as you are free to make mindful choices in support of your dream, so too are the knuckleheads in your life free to choose to make silly, unconscious choices every once in a while. The consequences of each choice will be felt either way.

Actions I Will Take Today to Boost My Mojo:

Gratitude Rant:

Personal Reflections:

329

By making consistent, conscious choices of empowerment and expansion, you will free yourself of fear, shame, and victimhood while filling yourself with joy, love, and power.
Don't those sound more appealing?

Actions I Will Take Today to Boost My Mojo:

Gratitude Rant:

Personal Reflections:

YOUR DAILY DOSE OF MOJO

330

Spirit is orchestrating your life like a Divine Play, opening exciting new doors of opportunity and giving you a rich palette of magical experiences in which to partake.

Actions I Will Take Today to Boost My Mojo:

Gratitude Rant:

Personal Reflections:

331

Celebrate the unexplained, special moments of magic that pepper your life. It is Spirit giving you little gifts on your journey.

Actions I Will Take Today to Boost My Mojo:

_____
_____
_____
_____
_____

Gratitude Rant:

_____
_____
_____
_____
_____

Personal Reflections:

_____
_____
_____
_____
_____

332

Magic takes place when we genuinely let go of the need to plan every last detail of our lives and surrender into the flow of the Divine.

Actions I Will Take Today to Boost My Mojo:
_____
_____
_____
_____
_____

Gratitude Rant:
_____
_____
_____
_____
_____

Personal Reflections:
_____
_____
_____
_____
_____

333

It's important to embrace the unexpected. The magic that results from something new entering our experience is Spirit giving us what we don't even know we want or need yet.

Actions I Will Take Today to Boost My Mojo:

_____
_____
_____
_____
_____

Gratitude Rant:

_____
_____
_____
_____
_____

Personal Reflections:

_____
_____
_____
_____
_____

334

We take a magician's trick at face value, experience the joy, and let go of the need to understand the how. When Spirit helps you on your journey, take it at face value, experience the benefit, and let go of any need to logically rationalize it. Just enjoy the magic!

Actions I Will Take Today to Boost My Mojo:

Gratitude Rant:

Personal Reflections:

335

Perform your own breed of magic show through your mindfulness: make your doubts disappear by waving your imaginary wand of power. Put every small thought, hesitation, and nagging fear in your top hat and make them go POOF! You don't need to hold onto them anymore.

Actions I Will Take Today to Boost My Mojo:

Gratitude Rant:

Personal Reflections:

336

Magic is at play all of the time when we are in pursuit of our dreams. We turn thoughts into things, intentions into money, and prayers into reality. We are constantly shifting energy into new forms, and Spirit gives us the power we need to deliver the
Greatest Show on Earth: our lives.

Actions I Will Take Today to Boost My Mojo:

_____
_____
_____
_____
_____

Gratitude Rant:

_____
_____
_____
_____
_____

Personal Reflections:

_____
_____
_____
_____
_____

337

When you are passionate about a goal, a cause, or a creative endeavor, you will find ways through, around, above, and below the natural resistance that you will encounter.

Actions I Will Take Today to Boost My Mojo:

Gratitude Rant:

Personal Reflections:

338

If you have lost your passion, then you have lost your drive to create the life you desire. Without passion, we merely exist; we don't truly live. The good news: it is easy to recover. Just ask your inner self what lights your heart on fire, then give yourself permission
to actually pursue it.

Actions I Will Take Today to Boost My Mojo:

Gratitude Rant:

Personal Reflections:

339

In a sea of the collective distraction, stress, and too much noise, it's easy for us to feel lost in the shuffle. Your passion, however, acts as a spotlight that gets you noticed and heard by others.

Actions I Will Take Today to Boost My Mojo:
_____
_____
_____
_____
_____

Gratitude Rant:
_____
_____
_____
_____
_____

Personal Reflections:
_____
_____
_____
_____
_____

340

If you don't know what your passion is,
start looking around for clues.
What are you known for?
How would you like spend your time?
How do people describe you?
Those nuggets of information point to
your passion that you
may not even be aware of yet.

Actions I Will Take Today to Boost My Mojo:

Gratitude Rant:

Personal Reflections:

341

Your passion may be a tiny ember in your heart that you have not allowed to grow. It's time to get that fire blazing! Breathe energy into that passion through your dreams and actions. When we serve from a place of passion, we accomplish so much more.

Actions I Will Take Today to Boost My Mojo:

_____
_____
_____
_____
_____

Gratitude Rant:

_____
_____
_____
_____
_____

Personal Reflections:

_____
_____
_____
_____
_____

342

It's OK to have a weird passion. (Mine is hoopdancing, for goodness sake!) Don't shy away from energizing your desires just because they may be odd to those around you. Their emotional response to your passion is irrelevant; only your opinion matters. Hoop on!

Actions I Will Take Today to Boost My Mojo:

Gratitude Rant:

Personal Reflections:

343

Sometimes our passions don't have to have a purpose, per se. They can merely be repositories of bliss that we partake in simply because we can. Life is meant to be enjoyed, not just tolerated. Your passion has value, simply because it brings you joy.

Actions I Will Take Today to Boost My Mojo:

_____
_____
_____
_____
_____

Gratitude Rant:

_____
_____
_____
_____
_____

Personal Reflections:

_____
_____
_____
_____
_____

YOUR DAILY DOSE OF MOJO

344

When you believe in you,
others will too.

Actions I Will Take Today to Boost My Mojo:

_____
_____
_____
_____

Gratitude Rant:

_____
_____
_____
_____

Personal Reflections:

_____
_____
_____
_____

345

One of my mom's philosophies on work was, "Fake it 'til you make it." Acting as if we already know or have something, will eventually bring it to fruition. If you are less than confident about something, fake it! You will soon find that you embody the very thing you pretended to be.

Actions I Will Take Today to Boost My Mojo:
_____
_____
_____
_____
_____

Gratitude Rant:
_____
_____
_____
_____
_____

Personal Reflections:
_____
_____
_____
_____
_____

346

Confidence comes from genuinely accepting ourselves, flaws and all. To be confident is to know that we are valued, amazing individuals with a wealth of gifts, regardless of the size of our thighs or the wrinkle factor. Authentic acceptance of our awesomeness is the greatest confidence booster around.

Actions I Will Take Today to Boost My Mojo:

Gratitude Rant:

Personal Reflections:

347

One of the sexiest things about someone is the confidence factor. When we are comfortable in our own skins, joy naturally emanates from us. When we emanate joy, others want to be around us. If you want to attract others in your life—for business, friendship or love—focus on truly loving yourself.

Actions I Will Take Today to Boost My Mojo:

Gratitude Rant:

Personal Reflections:

348

When we are teaching our kids, one of the most important things we can impart on them is self-respect. They will always run into things they don't know, but if they have a strong sense of confidence in who they are as people, they will get through any rough patch.

Actions I Will Take Today to Boost My Mojo:

Gratitude Rant:

Personal Reflections:

349

Confidence is not arrogance. It is a natural state of grace, knowing that you are fully embodying your God-given potential. Arrogance is a fearful state where you need to toot your own horn because you are afraid that you aren't being noticed or appreciated.

Actions I Will Take Today to Boost My Mojo:

Gratitude Rant:

Personal Reflections:

350

Be confident in your ability to change your circumstances if you so choose. Remember, when you are in alignment with your own power and in integration with Spirit, you can and will create the rich, rewarding life you want. You have everything you need.

Actions I Will Take Today to Boost My Mojo:

Gratitude Rant:

Personal Reflections:

351

Most of our pain stems from our unhealthy attachment to an outcome that never arrives.

Actions I Will Take Today to Boost My Mojo:

Gratitude Rant:

Personal Reflections:

YOUR DAILY DOSE OF MOJO

352

When we let go, we are free.

Actions I Will Take Today to Boost My Mojo:

_____
_____
_____
_____
_____

Gratitude Rant:

_____
_____
_____
_____
_____

Personal Reflections:

_____
_____
_____
_____
_____

353

We can't change those around us, so why do we get so attached to the notion? Life is what it is, and they are who they are. It is up to us to genuinely accept them as-is and let go of the need to change them. Either that, or we can decide to make a change for ourselves. Changing them is never an option.

Actions I Will Take Today to Boost My Mojo:

Gratitude Rant:

Personal Reflections:

354

A fine line exists between energizing a dream and attaching to an outcome. A teacher once suggested that I finish my prayers with, "Thank you, Spirit, for this or something better." The last phrase gives us permission to detach ourselves from the specifics of our dreams, and leave it up to Spirit to decide the details.

Actions I Will Take Today to Boost My Mojo:

Gratitude Rant:

Personal Reflections:

355

Our stress often stems from holding on too tightly to what we want a situation to be. We cry, whine, and yell, "Why can't it be the way I want it to be?" Let's release the grip of how we want things to be and trust that things are happening in the exact right way.

Actions I Will Take Today to Boost My Mojo:

Gratitude Rant:

Personal Reflections:

356

To detach yourself from an outcome is to flow freely on the current of Spirit. You don't need to paddle or fight against the waves.
Instead, just trust and surrender.
You'll enjoy the ride a lot more.

Actions I Will Take Today to Boost My Mojo:

Gratitude Rant:

Personal Reflections:

357

If you consistently feel drained after being around a particular person or environment for a period of time, you may want to consider consciously detaching from them. Just as barnacles latch onto other surfaces, energy vampires can latch onto us.

Actions I Will Take Today to Boost My Mojo:

_____
_____
_____
_____
_____

Gratitude Rant:

_____
_____
_____
_____
_____

Personal Reflections:

_____
_____
_____
_____
_____

358

When you say "Yes" more than you say "No," more possibilities will present themselves to you.
"No" shuts doors;
"Yes" opens them.

Actions I Will Take Today to Boost My Mojo:

Gratitude Rant:

Personal Reflections:

359

How do you know that something is impossible? Do you know it for an absolute fact? Or is it possible that something or someone could enter into the mix to help make it a reality? You never know what forces are at play in support of your dream, so don't automatically jump to "it's impossible."

Actions I Will Take Today to Boost My Mojo:

Gratitude Rant:

Personal Reflections:

YOUR DAILY DOSE OF MOJO

360

We often unknowingly contribute to someone's smallness by reciting, "He never does it right." or "She always messes things up." Our energy and language are powerful agents. Perceive all of those in your orbit as powerful beings and see the magic that takes place.

Actions I Will Take Today to Boost My Mojo:

Gratitude Rant:

Personal Reflections:

361

We don't even know what we don't know. Why limit our opportunities to only those things that we see and understand? Our job is not to figure it all out. Instead, we can look for the signs, trust in the Divine nudges, and boldly act in support of our Bigness.

Actions I Will Take Today to Boost My Mojo:
_____
_____
_____
_____
_____

Gratitude Rant:
_____
_____
_____
_____
_____

Personal Reflections:
_____
_____
_____
_____
_____

362

When you imagine your dream life, do you see it as possible? You may sometimes perceive it as improbable or unlikely, but don't ever see it as impossible. As long as you take another breath, your dream is possible.
You are a powerful force of creation.

Actions I Will Take Today to Boost My Mojo:

Gratitude Rant:

Personal Reflections:

363

Much more is in store for you!

Actions I Will Take Today to Boost My Mojo:
_____
_____
_____
_____
_____

Gratitude Rant:
_____
_____
_____
_____
_____

Personal Reflections:
_____
_____
_____
_____
_____

YOUR DAILY DOSE OF MOJO

364

Where others may live in a world of lack, limitation, and impossibility, you have the opportunity to live as freely and fully as you desire. You have the tools. You have the wisdom. You have the help. You have the passion.
You are remarkable.

Actions I Will Take Today to Boost My Mojo:

Gratitude Rant:

Personal Reflections:

365

Keep dreaming, keep taking action, and keep believing in yourself.

Actions I Will Take Today to Boost My Mojo:

_____
_____
_____
_____
_____

Gratitude Rant:

_____
_____
_____
_____
_____

Personal Reflections:

_____
_____
_____
_____
_____

ACKNOWLEDGMENTS

Thank you to the thousands of people who subscribed to my online Daily Dose of Mojo for so many years. Your stories of hope, growth, courage and transformation were the fuel I needed to bring this project to fruition. You are truly the embodiment of my teachings, and I am honored to be a part of your mindful living and working.

Thank you to my coaches, colleagues, and mentors in the National Speakers Association, especially my dear friends and Mastermind partners Kristen Brown of The Happy Hour Effect and Janel Anderson of Working Conversations. Your insights, support and gentle encouragement nudged me to bring my Daily Doses of Mojo into their full expression.

Thank you to my daughter Emma who always made time to listen to me and support me, despite the fact that she is fully immersed in the drama of adolescence. She is my reason for being, and I am grateful to be her mother (even with her occasional eye-rolling antics.)

Finally, I would like to express my deep, profound gratitude to my best friend Jean. This incredible woman has stood by me through every conceivable challenge, both personal and professional, and never let me forget how important it was for me to share my wisdom with the world. My success as a speaker, author and performer has Jean's imprint all over it. Our countless walk-n-talks gave me the vision, clarity, and mojo I needed to take my dreams to reality. *I love you, Jean.*

ABOUT THE AUTHOR

Theresa Rose is a nationally acclaimed business and motivational speaker, award-winning author of four books, entrepreneurial mentor and hardcore hoopdancer who helps individuals and organizations increase engagement and expand into their fullest potential. Prior to launching her speaking career, Theresa was a senior manager of marketing and product development for a Fortune 100 company, a management consultant specializing in process improvement and rapid product implementation, and the owner of a cool, hippy-dippy alternative healing center in Florida.

Theresa was named a top five finalist in the "So You Think You Can Speak?" competition and delivered an electrifying TEDxTalk called "The Hoop Revolution" at TEDxSarasota. She was honored to serve as the President of the Minnesota Chapter of the National Speakers Association, the premier association for professional speaking. Theresa combines humor, authenticity and her visually stunning hoop performances with rock-solid, actionable content to help organizations cultivate stronger leaders, improve sales and service, and re-engage the zombie workforce.

The stage is Theresa's natural habitat, her daughter Emma is the light in her life (and sometimes her greatest challenge!), and her beloved hula hoop is her favorite teacher. For more information on Theresa, visit TheresaRose.com.

BOOK THERESA

If you are looking for a speaker that will help your organization *Sell More, Lead Stronger and Live Better*, Theresa is the speaker for you. Her electrifying presentations deliver the energy, content, value and ROI you need to make a lasting impact.

- Cultivate and leverage the power of emotional value that moves your customers to gladly part with their money.
- Execute Mindful Marketing that focuses on compelling storytelling that leads to increased conversion.
- Create a joy-infused culture that gets your team to want to come to work every day—and actually work.

Theresa taps into her extensive background as an organizational leader, sales and marketing executive, and electrifying performer to deliver customized programs that are perfectly tied to your organizational mission and event theme.

Here are some of the ways Theresa can add value to your next event:

Vegas-style entertainment with captivating stories and infectious comedy

Memorable key takeaways designed to be leveraged long after the event is over

Master of Ceremonies, Panel Facilitation and Breakout Sessions

---

Invest in Theresa for your conference, sales team event or leadership training today!

Theresa@TheresaRose.com – 952-456-1670

Made in the USA
Middletown, DE
19 June 2016